D0105078

MYTHOLOGY

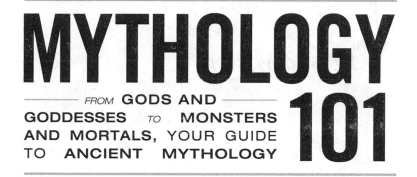

FROM **GODS AND GODDESSES** TO **MONSTERS AND MORTALS,** YOUR GUIDE TO **ANCIENT MYTHOLOGY**

101

KATHLEEN SEARS

A adamsmedia
Avon, Massachusetts

Published by
Adams Media, a division of F+W Media, Inc.
57 Littlefield Street, Avon, MA 02322. U.S.A.
www.adamsmedia.com

Contains material adapted and abridged from *The Everything® Classical Mythology Book* by Lesley Bolton, copyright © 2002 by F+W Media, Inc., ISBN 10: 1-58062-653-X, ISBN 13: 978-1-58062-653-8; and *The Everything® Classical Mythology Book, 2nd Edition* by Nancy Conner, copyright © 2010, 2002 by F+W Media, Inc., ISBN 10: 1-4405-0240-4, ISBN 13: 978-1-4405-0240-8.

ISBN 10: 1-4405-7332-8
ISBN 13: 978-1-4405-7332-3
eISBN 10: 1-4405-7333-6
eISBN 13: 978-1-4405-7333-0

Printed in the United States of America.

10   9   8   7   6   5   4   3   2   1

Cover images © Clipart.com. Interior illustrations by Barry Littmann. Additional illustrations reprinted with permission from Dover Publications, Inc.

This book is available at quantity discounts for bulk purchases.
For information, please call 1-800-289-0963.

CONTENTS

INTRODUCTION

Many years have passed since the Greeks and Romans worshiped the gods and goddesses of Mount Olympus—centuries, in fact. The ancient characters you may have heard of before, like mighty Zeus, monstrous Medusa, and seductive Aphrodite, originate from myths dating back to 900 B.C. So why study mythology today? In short, classical mythology has impacted history, literature, culture, and life across the Western world and beyond; truly, it has shaped the ancient world *and* the modern world, and continues to impact contemporary life today. For example, the language you speak has been impacted by classical mythology: Conceited people are *narcissists*; your enemy's weakness is his *Achilles heel*; you may have experienced a dreamlike state of *hypnosis*; and you've used an *atlas* to gaze at the world. The months of the year trace their names to Roman mythology; the constellations have their origins in myth, too. Some of the world's most famous writers and philosophers detailed the quarrels of the gods and the lives of men, including Homer, Sophocles, Virgil, and Ovid. This list may be impressive, but it merely scratches the surface of what classical mythology has to offer.

The ancient Greeks and Romans used myths to explain the wonders of the world, including the rise of humanity, the causes of natural phenomena, and the origin of the Earth and the universe. Myths not only shared stories of creation—they wove narratives of love, betrayal, war, lust, jealousy, loyalty, and tragedy across many centuries, told through tales of mighty gods, noble heroes, and terrifying monsters. And the myths aren't limited to the tales of gods of men alone. You'll discover some of the most creative beings ever recorded in history, including the aggressive Centaurs, half man and half horse; the irresistible Sirens, luring wayward sailors to their deaths; and the *original* monsters, like the Minotaur, the Sphinx, the Chimera, and the Cyclopes. You will also find the stories behind some of history's most famous adventures and battles, including the Trojan War, Odysseus's epic journey, and Oedipus's tragic life story. Plus, you'll meet the most popular gods and goddesses in Greek mythology (and their Roman counterparts), including war-loving Ares, wise Athena, jealous Hera, elusive Hades, furious Poseidon, and their heroic mortal counterparts, like Jason, Perseus, Heracles, and Theseus.

Mythology 101 will guide you through the most glorious (and completely terrifying) tales the ancient world had to offer. And don't worry; we've highlighted the Greek and Roman myths with their own icons, **G** and **R**, so you'll know the exact origins of every account. In addition, you'll find family trees for the Greek and Roman gods, so you can easily remember the "who's who" of the ancient world. No matter what type of story you enjoy most—romance, adventure, mystery, horror—these ancient legends will have something for all your interests. Whether you're new to the gods and want to learn more about their stories, supplementing a literature or history course, or brushing up on what you learned in high school, this fun and comprehensive guide to gods is the perfect introduction to Greek and Roman mythology.

DEFINING A MYTH

Adventures of Passion, Tragedy, War, and Heroism

G **R**

A myth, defined simply, is a fictitious story or half-truth, but it goes much deeper than that. Scholars of mythology have struggled to pinpoint an exact definition that encompasses all of the attributes contained within a myth. It's funny how such a small word both defines and gives purpose to lofty ideas, such as the meaning of life. It's no wonder an accurate definition has not been settled on!

In popular usage, the word *myth* usually refers to a fictitious story or a half-truth. For example, you might see a report in the media that uses *myth* for some commonly held belief that the reporter wants to prove is untrue. But myths go much deeper than false beliefs or made-up stories. Scholars of mythology have struggled to agree on an exact definition, one that encompasses everything myth can mean. Myths may deal with questions of origins—who you are and where you came from. They may teach values or attempt to explain natural phenomena. Myths are often intertwined with religion, and some look ahead to the end of time.

This book focuses on Greek and Roman mythology, but these are not the only myths. Other cultures—such as Japanese, Native American, Indian, Chinese, Norse, African, Celtic, Aboriginal, and Egyptian peoples—have their own myths. Although the stories may be wildly different, all myths share certain characteristics. Looking at these similarities offers a starting point for developing a working definition of myth.

CREATING MYTHS,
EXPLAINING PHENOMENA

The myth has several characteristics that set it apart from other kinds of stories. One characteristic is how a myth is created. Unlike most works of fiction, myths are not the creation of a single author. A myth evolves as it's told, over and over again. Scholars explain that the mythology of a culture is created through the oral renderings of its people. Someone tells a story, and then the audience tells it again, and their listeners tell it again—and on it goes. Because myths are told and retold, passed from one person to the next, there is often more than one version of the same story.

A myth is a religious story that involves a higher power or entity. The gods, goddesses, and other supernatural beings who appear in myths are worshiped or revered. Within the culture that created it, the myth is considered sacred and believed to be true.

A myth may attempt to explain the unknown, such as how the universe or Earth was created. It also attempts to answer the broad, fundamental questions all people ask themselves about the meaning and purpose of human existence.

Any individual myth is part of a larger mythology, a group of stories that belong to one culture. The myths that make up a mythology may be tied together by shared characters (such as the gods and goddesses involved), historical events (such as the Trojan War), or common themes (such as love and sex). A culture's mythology contains socially accepted truths that provide a sense of identity, shared values, and purpose.

These characteristics comprise the essential elements of a myth. In addition, a few other elements—not necessarily essential to all myths—may appear. For example, many myths highlight activities that break the laws of nature: People change into inanimate objects, the dead rise and live again, and so forth. Also, myths often convey different planes of existence and the interaction between them—heaven and hell, for example, or the future and the past.

ANCIENT QUESTIONS

The ancients, just like us, hungered for knowledge. Most wanted explanations for what they considered to be phenomena they encountered in their daily lives. Others went beyond that and wanted reasons for the structure of the universe. Regardless of the importance or size of the question, a curiosity drove them to begin asking questions. And myths were formed to provide explanation for these otherwise unanswerable questions.

Myths not only take on the challenge of tackling these colossal questions, but also venture to answer the more everyday wonderings, including:

- The origin of certain constellations
- Why the sun disappears at night
- Why certain creatures behave the way they do (for instance, why the spider weaves a web)
- How the evils—sickness, death, grief—were released upon the world
- How fire came to man
- The changing of the seasons

The Greeks and Romans answered these questions through myths. This explanatory element of the myth is quite important to its structure. Just like any other religion, classical mythology sought to provide definitive answers to these ever-looming questions.

A STORY FOR EVERY READER

If you enjoy stories of war and bravery in battle, you'll be glad to know that classical mythology is full of exciting battle scenes. The ancients were fierce warriors, and the myths describe their fights in great detail. The story of the Trojan War, for example, contains many graphic descriptions of fighting.

Horror fans will find a fascinating variety of monsters in classical mythology—including some you never dreamed might be lurking under your bed. From Typhon, who had a hundred serpentine heads, to the Minotaur, who ate children, the monsters of classical mythology will give you chills and might even keep you up at night.

Adventure, tragedy, battles, and monsters are just the beginning. You'll also encounter tales of witchcraft and revenge, murder and mystery, crime and punishment, and passionate love and seduction. Love and sex play a major role in mythology, including stories of scandalous affairs—such as the one between Aphrodite and Ares—and stories of true love—such as the myth of Perseus and Andromeda.

With such a wide variety of tales to choose from, classical mythology is guaranteed to have something for everyone!

THE GREEK STORYTELLERS

A Blind Bard, an Epic Performer, and Other Ancient Authors

Ⓖ

Mythology doesn't come from a single source. Myths develop as they're told and retold, passed from one storyteller to another, from one generation to the next. This section surveys some of the most important mythmakers of ancient Greece. These poets, dramatists, and other storytellers were the best-selling authors of their time. Because their works were popular and valued, they were recorded and preserved.

HOMER: THE GREATEST POET OF THE ANCIENT WORLD

You will never study classical mythology without hearing the name of Homer. Homer is regarded as not only the greatest poet of the ancient world, but also one of the greatest—and certainly one of the most influential—artists of the literary world. But did Homer truly exist? This question has been debated among scholars, historians, and the common man alike for centuries. What is not argued, though, is the prominence of the *Iliad* and the *Odyssey*, literary tomes attributed to Homer.

Several theories assert that Homer wasn't the single author of all the works attributed to him. Some scholars even doubt that he existed at all. One theory posits that several different people composed these poems, and the result was later attributed to Homer.

Other theories suggest that Homer composed the first part of the *Odyssey* and that one or more other bards concluded the poem.

Ancient Entertainment

Homer's epic poems, the *Iliad* and the *Odyssey*, each run approximately 12,000 lines. To perform either poem in its entirety would take several evenings. To the ancients, listening to an epic poem was an exciting way to spend an evening. These two poems tell of the Trojan War and its aftermath. The Greek victory over Troy was a defining moment for the Greeks and the catalyst for the foundation of Rome. These epics became an integral part of Greek culture. In fact, the Greeks were said to have introduced the study of these works into their schools around 400 B.C.

Why is there this skepticism? The works of Homer have been studied for centuries. Scholars who have compared the *Iliad*, the *Odyssey*, and other poems attributed to Homer have found significant differences. Others note that Homeric works blend different dialects, even though people typically speak only one dialect. Although the differences among Homeric works raise questions about who composed them, "Homer" still created the foundation for classical mythology—whether he was a single man or several different authors.

HESIOD: SHROUDED IN MYSTERY

Hesiod is another important Greek poet. Often called the father of Greek didactic poetry, Hesiod probably lived some time after Homer. Unlike Homer's epic poetry, which typically narrates heroic deeds and important events, didactic poetry tells a story to teach a moral lesson.

Like Homer, Hesiod is mysterious, but scholars do know a bit more about his life. The best guess is that he lived sometime around 700 B.C. in the village of Ascra in central Greece. According to his poems, he tended sheep in his youth, becoming a farmer after his father died. Although he was poor, Hesiod wasn't a typical peasant. Yet his works clearly show the perspective of a farmer who lived a difficult life.

While tending his flock one day, the young Hesiod was visited by the Muses, goddesses of literature and the arts. They appeared to him in a mist and gave him a poet's staff and a poet's voice. Then they told him to use these gifts to spread the word about the gods. Hesiod did as he was told, even competing in poetry contests. The results of this mystical visitation were the famous works *Theogony* and *Works and Days*, as well as several lesser-known poems.

As with Homer, scholars debate whether Hesiod was the sole author of his works. But there is general agreement that Hesiod was an actual person and that he authored most of *Theogony* and *Works and Days*. Only parts of these works are suspected of having been added later by other poets.

Theogony fulfilled the Muses' command by telling the history of the gods. Beginning with creation, this poem provides a foundation on which to build the stories of the gods and goddesses. *Theogony* explains the origin of the universe, the gods, and the world. *Works and Days*, a poem of about 800 lines, is framed as a disagreement between Hesiod and his brother, Perses, over their late father's estate. *Works and Days* is filled with fables and myths as the two brothers debate the issue.

AESCHYLUS: SOLDIER, PERFORMER, PLAYWRIGHT

The next important period for mythology was the fifth century B.C., when Greece experienced a flowering of the theater. During this period, three Greek playwrights rose to fame for their tragic plays. The first of these tragedians was Aeschylus, who wrote more than ninety plays and is sometimes called the father of tragedy.

Historians know several facts about Aeschylus. He was born into an aristocratic family near Athens around 525 B.C., served as a soldier in the Persian Wars, and became a celebrated tragedian. He participated numerous times in the Great Dionysia, part of a festival honoring Dionysus, the Greek god of wine.

Competition at the Great Dionysia

For this festival, three dramatists each created three tragedies and a satyr play (a short play featuring drunkenness, sexuality, and practical jokes), which were performed and judged at the celebration. His first competition is thought to have taken place around 499 B.C., with his first victory in 484 B.C. From then on, Aeschylus won first prize in nearly every competition (although he was bested once by his protégé Sophocles).

Aeschylus is thought to have written ninety plays during his lifetime, approximately eighty of which are known from the bits and pieces that have survived. However, only seven of his plays, all tragedies, remain intact today: *The Persians, Seven Against Thebes, The Suppliants, Agamemnon, The Libation Bearers, The Eumenides* (the latter three make up the famous trilogy the *Oresteia*), and *Prometheus Bound.*

A major theme of these tragedies is justice. Aeschylus believed that the gods and goddesses sometimes resented mortals' attempts to attain greatness, which they saw as hubris (excessive pride). The deities often pursued justice by tricking a person into causing his own downfall through pride. The unjust were not always punished directly; sometimes, punishment fell upon a culprit's descendants.

Aeschylus died around 455 B.C. in Gela, Sicily, at the age of sixty-nine. The cause of his death is unknown, although a rumor (thought to have been started by a comic writer) claimed that Aeschylus was killed when an eagle dropped a tortoise on his bald head. Regardless of how he died, Aeschylus was honored with a public funeral at which sacrifices and performances were carried out.

SOPHOCLES: THE MOST SUCCESSFUL TRAGEDIAN

Sophocles, a student of Aeschylus, is considered by many to be the most successful of the Greek tragedians. Like Aeschylus, Sophocles lived during a time of many wars, including the Persian Wars (546–479 B.C.) and the Peloponnesian War (431–404 B.C.). Sophocles's work was influenced by this strife.

Born into a wealthy family in 496 B.C., Sophocles was sent to Athens to receive a good education. He studied military technique, science, mathematics, philosophy, government, law, astronomy, and the arts. It is widely believed that Sophocles studied under Aeschylus.

Sophocles was a talented and popular man who excelled in nearly everything he did. He was handsome and widely respected. He held many public offices and was a patron of the arts. Sophocles also took part in the Great Dionysia, winning his first victory in 468 B.C. at the age of twenty-nine. He went on to win this competition eighteen times (some sources say twenty-four times).

Oedipus

Thanks to Sophocles, the character of Oedipus is widely known. Sophocles began with the basic myth of Oedipus and expanded on it, creating three of his most famous tragedies: *Oedipus the King*, *Oedipus at Colonus*, and *Antigone*. The gods also appear throughout his works. Sophocles saw the gods as higher beings, and humans as subject to their decisions. If the gods felt a man should be punished, for example, he was indeed brought to justice.

During his long life, Sophocles wrote an estimated 123 plays. Today, only seven have survived intact: *Oedipus the King*, *Oedipus at Colonus*, *Antigone*, *Ajax*, *The Trachiniae*, *Philoctetes*, and *Electra*. Each of these plays is built on a foundation of mythology. War and conflict are frequent themes in his plays, and this conflict causes his characters much pain and suffering. The plays suggest that it is through this pain and suffering that people become more human.

Sophocles died around 409 B.C. at the age of ninety. As with Aeschylus, unlikely rumors circulated about the cause of his death. One rumor humorously claimed he died during an attempt to recite a long sentence from one of his plays without stopping to take a breath; another said he choked on some grapes. However he died, it is certain that Sophocles lived a long, full life and made a significant contribution to Greek literature and our understanding of mythology.

EURIPIDES: A CONTROVERSIAL PHILOSOPHER

The last of the great Greek tragedians was Euripides, known today for his philosophical plays and strong female characters. Euripides constantly questioned all that the Greeks held sacred. For this reason, he was controversial in his day; in fact, he was openly disliked and criticized during his lifetime.

Euripides was born around 480 B.C. on the island of Salamis. Little is known about his background, although he was obviously well educated, which suggests that his family was wealthy. It is likely that he studied the same broad range of subjects as Sophocles, but Euripides developed a strong passion for philosophy; he questioned cherished assumptions and was openly skeptical of the gods and goddesses.

Euripides started writing plays around the age of eighteen. He, too, competed in the Great Dionysia, beginning in 455 B.C., but he didn't win until he was about forty years old. Euripides is thought to have written ninety-two plays, although only seventeen tragedies have survived. (Notice, however, that this is more than the surviving plays of Aeschylus and Sophocles combined.)

Many Mythological Plays

The plays of Euripides that you can read today are *Andromache*, *Hecuba*, *Iphigenia at Aulis*, *Bacchae*, *Alcestis*, *Medea*, *The Children of Heracles*, *Hippolytus*, *The Suppliants*, *Electra*, *The Madness of Heracles*, *Ion*, *The Trojan Women*, *Iphigenia among the Taurians*, *The Phoenician Women*, *Helen*, and *Orestes*. Like the other Greek tragedians, Euripides uses mythology as a foundation for his plays.

As a philosopher, Euripides appreciated realism, and his plays reflect this. His works introduce protagonists—main characters—who are common everyday people. Even the deities function on a common level; people often equal them in importance. Euripides also emphasized strong female characters, making them protagonists who received as much recognition as the traditional war hero. Euripides saw humans as complex, multifaceted beings. He thought it was essential that people recognized both sides of themselves—body and mind—instead of pretending that people are primarily rational or godlike.

One of the things that gained Euripides renown was his library, believed to be one of the first ever put together by a private individual. Although he lived in Athens for most of his life, he retired to Macedonia, where he died around 406 B.C. at the age of seventy-seven.

ROMAN MYTHMAKERS

Virgil and Ovid: Epic Poets of the Augustan Age

Ⓡ

The Greeks weren't the only ones to have great poets of mythology within their culture. During the Augustan Age of Rome, two poets stood out amongst the mythmakers, poets who are often compared to Homer and Hesiod—Virgil and Ovid. These two Roman poets are held in the highest esteem for bringing immortality to Roman mythology.

VIRGIL

Virgil, whose full name was Publius Vergilius Maro, was born on October 15, 70 B.C. in the village of Andes. His father, a wealthy farmer, sent his son to Cremona, Milan, and Rome for his education. Virgil studied both Greek and Roman literature, as well as law, rhetoric, and philosophy. Legend has it that Virgil's father wanted him to become a lawyer. After arguing his first case, however, Virgil decided that the law wasn't for him and turned his attention to philosophy and poetry.

Virgil was a popular poet who had influential friends, including his patron, the Roman emperor Augustus, and various important political and literary figures. Although Virgil lived for many years in Rome, he never abandoned his love of the countryside, a love that is evident in his poetry.

Virgil is best known for the *Aeneid*. This epic poem, which tells the story of the origins of Rome, follows the Trojan hero Aeneas after the fall of Troy, as he travels and then settles in a new land, where he founds a new race: the Romans. The poem introduces all of the great characters of ancient Roman mythology, mortal and immortal alike, including Dido, Romulus, Jupiter, and Venus, to name just a few. This timeless classic has inspired many authors over the centuries.

Virgil's Other Essential Works

Although the *Aeneid* is Virgil's most famous work, he also wrote other important poems. His earliest work is a collection of ten short pastoral poems entitled *Eclogues*, which show the lives and loves of shepherds in idealized rural settings. Another major work, *Georgics*, reflects Virgil's love of the Italian countryside (and may have served as political propaganda). In this work, Virgil exhorts farmers to go back to the land and preserve the agricultural lifestyle.

Virgil was essentially Rome's national poet. His works are central to the study of Roman history and culture. Thanks to the enduring popularity of Virgil's poems, today's scholars know a great deal about Roman mythology.

In 19 B.C., Virgil was traveling to Greece to visit some of the sites described in the *Aeneid* as he revised that poem. En route, he contracted a fever and died on September 21. The dying Virgil asked that his remains be taken to Naples and buried near his villa there. His bones were believed to offer protection to the city of Naples.

OVID

Rome's other great poet, Ovid, is renowned for his fantastic storytelling abilities. Ovid was a hit with not only the ancients, but also with readers of today. It is said that Ovid is read more than any other ancient poet, even his predecessor Virgil. His works have influenced and inspired famous writers of both Roman and English literature. And most importantly, he provided us with several of the very best sources of classical mythology.

Ovid was born on March 20, 43 B.C., as Publius Ovidius Naso. He was born in the small country town of Sulmona, which is about 90 miles east of Rome. He came from a fairly affluent and respectable family, and his father sent him and his older brother to Rome for their education.

From Knighthood to a Poet's Society

Ovid became a member of the Roman knightly class and used this position to travel around before officially taking on any duties. However, once he did settle down and take up some of the duties necessary for his career in public life, he found he didn't have the stomach for it. Instead he abandoned his post, settled in Rome, and took up with a society of poets. Obviously, he made the right decision, for once he began producing, he immediately became a great success.

Ovid wrote several works, though by far the most popular is the narrative poem *Metamorphoses*, which is often called "the major treasury of classical mythology." Consisting of approximately 12,000 lines, this poem is a collection of Roman mythological stories. It covers everything from the creation theory to the death of Julius Caesar. Needless to say, this work is an amazing masterpiece, full of impressive Roman mythology.

Now, you'd think that a project that size would take one an entire lifetime to complete, but Ovid had time for several other compositions as well. *The Amores*, a series of poems describing a love affair, were his first published poems. Keeping with these passionate lines is *Heroides*, which is a series of imaginary love letters written by mythological characters to their lovers. And of course we can't forget *Fasti*, which describes the various religious festivals upheld by the Romans on a month-to-month basis. Unfortunately, only the first six books—the first six months—have survived.

Ovid enjoyed immense popularity during his lifetime and his popularity is still going strong today. However, his life wasn't entirely full of glory. In A.D. 8 he was exiled to Tomis on the Black Sea. The reasons behind his banishment are still a mystery, but rumor states that it involved an adulterous affair with the emperor's granddaughter. He died in A.D. 17, still begging to be allowed to return to Rome.

CHAOS, PROMETHEUS, AND THE BIRTH OF MAN

Or, the Ancients' Version of the Big Bang Theory

G

Today, numerous theories exist about how the universe was created. The ancients also wondered how the universe was created, and their attempts at explaining this creation formed the basis of various myths. One idea was constant, however: The universe emerged from chaos.

IMPOSING ORDER UPON DISORDER

Before there was Earth or sky or seas, all of the elements of the universe were one, and this oneness was called Chaos. Chaos was a shapeless void of confusion, but it held the seeds of an organized universe. Contained within Chaos the elements—earth, sky, sea—were jumbled together; no one element had an identity. Earth didn't have its shape, the sky didn't have air, and the sea was not watery.

The elements fought constantly until an unknown force put an end to the disorder. This force is not explicitly identified in the myths. Regardless, the elements were separated—heaven from earth, sea from sky, heat from cold, and so on—and this separation imposed the order needed to create the universe.

Once separated, the elements still needed shape and definition. According to one popular myth, an unnamed force (some call it the Creator) first gave shape to Earth. The Creator designated water to its appropriate places; he then raised the mountains, smoothed out the plains, and shoveled out the valleys, distributing forests, rocky terrain, and fertile fields. Next came the sky: The Creator spread out the air like a blank canvas. He added clouds, thunder, lightning, and winds. The stars, however, he drew from the confines of darkness.

After setting up the sky and Earth, the Creator added the fish to the seas, the birds to the air, and beasts to land. Not all of the beasts were created at this time—humanity still did not exist.

THE UNIONS

Uranus, said to have been born to Gaia in her sleep, mates with his mother (yes, incest permeates classical mythology) to create the rest of Earth's elements, such as the waters, forestry, and the beasts. Uranus and Gaia also produced other children, including the Titans and Titanesses, the Cyclopes, and the Hundred-Handed Ones.

Nyx mated with Erebus to produce Hemera (Day) and Aether (Air). Nyx also bore several other children. These are Thanatos (Death), Hypnos (Sleep), Moros (Doom), Nemesis (Retribution), Oizys (Pain), Momus (Sarcasm), Eris (Strife), the Keres (the female spirits of death), Geras (Old Age), Oneiroi (Dreams), and the Moirai (Fates). Obviously, she was quite busy. The unions did not end there, but this explanation helps to define the elements of the universe a little bit further.

FINALLY . . . THE CREATION OF MAN

So far, both myths discussed have set the stage for the creation of humanity. The ancient myths vary on exactly how people were created. One myth, popular with Greeks and Romans alike, states that man simply sprang up from the earth. Remember the seeds of the universe buried in Chaos? This myth contains a similar idea about humanity: The seeds of man were buried in the earth. These seeds produced men, who were considered the children of Gaia.

PROMETHEUS: SCULPTOR OF CLAY, CREATOR OF MAN?

When considering the ancient myths surrounding mankind's creation, Prometheus is often given credit for this monumental task. Another theory is that Prometheus was the creator of man. Prometheus was a Titan and one of Gaia's many grandchildren. Prometheus and his brother Epimetheus were given the task of not only creating man, but also of giving the other beasts of Earth protection. Epimetheus took it upon himself to present the beasts with gifts of preservation and Prometheus was to supervise his work. Therefore, Epimetheus is credited with giving the turtles their shells, the leopards their spots, and the bears their claws.

When it came time to create man, Prometheus performed this task himself, using earth and clay as his materials. He kneaded this with water and fashioned the form of man, which was molded in the likeness of the gods. But the first man was not what we know as the man of today. The mortal man went through several stages before reaching the final desired effect.

FIRE: A GIFT OF STRENGTH AND PROTECTION

Epimetheus did such a good job of distributing gifts that by the time he was finished with his task, all the gifts of protection were accounted for—except for man's gift.

Prometheus decided that man also needed a gift of protection, one that went beyond all the others—and that gift was fire. But Zeus, ruler of the gods, was quite angry with mankind and refused to give them this fire. Prometheus was adamant though and resolved to steal fire from the heavens. Prometheus bestowed the gift of fire unto mankind.

A Risky Quest for Mankind

According to one account, Prometheus stole fire from the forge of Hephaestus, the smith of the gods. Another account states that he stole the fire from the wheels of Helios's (the sun's) chariot and concealed it in the stalk of a fennel plant. Regardless of how it happened, the quest was successful.

When Zeus looked down upon the Earth at night and saw it shining with firelight, his anger shook the heavens. He sent for his servants and ordered them to arrest Prometheus. The punishment of Prometheus was rather severe. Zeus ordered that Prometheus be bound by steel chains to a rock far from mankind. Zeus then sent an eagle to feed on his liver every day. The liver would regenerate every night. Vowing to never release Prometheus, Zeus left him to endure this torturous punishment.

THE ORDERED UNIVERSE: SUN, MOON, AND DAWN

A Handsome God, a Mysterious Goddess, and Their Tart of a Sister

Ⓖ

If you read about the creation of the universe, you may have noticed quite a few elements missing. For example, there is day, but no sun; there is night, but no moon. Dawn is the natural transition from night to day, but the ancient Greeks believed these deities appeared after the world's original offspring. The sun, moon, and dawn came later, born of the Titans.

THE SUN

Helios, god of the sun, was considered a lesser god. Even so, the other deities held him in great esteem. Helios was a handsome god who was responsible for giving daylight to Earth by driving his chariot of fire, pulled by four flaming steeds, across the sky from east to west. Night would fall as Helios crossed the western horizon, and it lasted as long as it took him to return to the East. Later myths claim that Helios made his way back to the East in a huge golden cup that floated along the river Oceanus, which encircled the world.

THE MOON

Selene, the moon, was Helios's sister. She also drove a chariot across the sky, though hers was made of silver and pulled by two horses. Selene was responsible for moonlight that shone through the night.

Not much else is known about Selene. The myths state that she was beautiful and famous for her love affairs. It was said that Pan, god of shepherds and flocks, tried to seduce her with either a beautiful fleece or a herd of white oxen—the myths vary. Selene also had an affair with Zeus, bearing him a daughter named Pandia.

Selene's most famous love affair was with Endymion, who may have been a shepherd, a hunter, or even a king. All versions of this myth agree, however, that Endymion was extremely handsome. Selene looked down upon him as he slept and fell instantly in love.

She descended from the heavens and made love to Endymion in his dreams. Some myths claim she bore him fifty daughters. At Selene's request, Zeus offered Endymion one wish. He wished for eternal youth—and some say for eternal sleep, as well, so he could continue to experience his amorous dreams—and was granted both sleep and immortality.

THE DAWN

Eos, the dawn, was Helios's other sister. Every morning, Eos would rise from her golden throne, open the gates of heaven, and announce the coming of the sun. She also accompanied Helios in his journey across the sky. Some myths say she rode alongside him in his chariot of fire; others say she rode in her own chariot in front of Helios, announcing his arrival all day long.

More Gods to Love

Many other deities represent the elements of the universe, though these lesser gods and goddesses aren't prominent in the myths. For example, there were 3,000 river gods and 3,000 ocean goddesses, not to mention the various demi-deities of the forests and mountains.

Eos's love life was even more famous than that of her sister, Selene. It would take hours to relate the tales of all her lovers. Eos's many unions resulted in some well-known children. She was the mother of the Winds: Boreas (North), Notus (South), and Zephyrus (West). She also gave birth to Eosphorus (the Morning Star) and all the other stars in the heavens.

PANDORA'S BOX

Woman: The Greatest Sculpture Ever Created—with a Catch

G

After Prometheus created man, he gave man the gift of fire—deliberately disobeying Zeus's rule. Even after punishing Prometheus for his insolence, Zeus was unhappy with the strength men had gained from the gift of fire. Therefore, he devised a scheme to inflict a powerful weakness upon men. Enter the woman. Until this time, according to the myths, mortal women did not exist.

Zeus ordered Hephaestus to fashion a woman from clay and water. The result was the greatest sculpture ever created. Just as man had been molded in the image of the gods, woman was molded in the image of the goddesses. As if this weren't enough, every deity contributed to Hephaestus's creation. Woman was given beauty, along with lust, splendid clothes, lustrous jewelry, and the gifts of music, grace, dexterity, and charm. In addition, woman was given the arts of seduction, deceit, and guile. These traits combined to create a dangerous temptress that man would be unable to resist. Her name was Pandora.

ZEUS'S GIFT, PANDORA'S MISTAKE

As his gift to mankind, Zeus ordered Hermes, the messenger of the gods, to deliver Pandora to Epimetheus. Awestruck by her beauty and charm, Epimetheus accepted Pandora as his bride, even though his brother Prometheus had warned him to not accept gifts from Zeus.

The ancient myths vary in the telling of Pandora's Box. One myth says that the gods gave Pandora a sealed jar and told her it was a gift to man. They did not tell her, however, what the jar held, and it wasn't long before her curiosity got the better of her. Pandora opened the jar and out flew the plagues of mankind: disease, pain, sorrow, insanity, envy, and death. Hastily replacing the lid, Pandora trapped hope, which was all that remained in the jar.

An Ancient Warning

The myth of Pandora's Box gave rise to a modern expression that describes a dangerous situation best left alone. If someone ever tells you that a situation is "a real Pandora's box," they're saying that the situation is likely to lead to trouble and confusion.

Another myth states that all the evils of the world were kept in a jar or box in the house of Epimetheus (whether this container belonged to Epimetheus or Prometheus is unknown). Overcome by curiosity, Pandora snuck into the room and removed the lid. Again, out poured all the ills of mankind, leaving behind only hope, which did not escape.

Still other versions of Pandora's myth say that the box contained only good things: blessings that were a wedding present from Zeus. In these versions, Pandora's curiosity again overcame her and she opened the box carelessly. All of the blessings escaped and returned to the heavens, except for hope. With the loss of most of the blessings, humanity had to endure all the hardships and evils of the world with only hope as a consolation.

Whichever version of her myth you prefer, Pandora's curiosity left humanity virtually defenseless against the difficulties that plague human life—and so Zeus got his revenge.

GAIA (EARTH) AND PONTUS

Mother Earth, and Her Son the Sea

Ⓖ

Gaia (Mother Earth) was part of the original offspring during creation. She had a huge responsibility to the universe, being the Earth and all, but above all else, she was a mother.

FIVE CHILDREN WITH PONTUS

According to the myth describing the world's creation from Chaos, Gaia gave birth to three children without the aid of a man. One of these was Pontus, the Sea. Gaia, although quite busy creating elements for the universe, took time out to then mate with Pontus. This union produced five children: Ceto, Eurybia, Nereus, Thaumas, and Phorcys.

LOVELY CETO, GODDESS OF SEA MONSTERS

Ceto was considered to be the deity of large marine beasts. The Greeks use her name informally to refer to sea monsters. Ceto married her brother, Phorcys. Together they produced several children:

- **The Graeae:** These three daughters were born as old women, never able to enjoy the freshness of youth. Their names were Deino, Enyo, and Pemphredo. The sisters were always portrayed together in the myths, and they weren't the prettiest of sights. Between them they had only one eye and one tooth, which they shared in turns. They lived in darkness away from the sunlight (some myths say they lived in a deep cave).

- **The Gorgons:** These three daughters were even less to look at than their sisters. They were monsters with snakes for hair, tusks, bronze claws, wings, and a stare that could turn men to stone. Both mortals and immortals feared these creatures. Only two of the Gorgons were immortal—Euryale and Stheno. The third and most recognizable to us, Medusa, was mortal.

- Yet another monster of a daughter, **Echidna** had the body of a beautiful woman and instead of legs, a serpent's tail. She is best known in classical mythology for giving birth to several monstrous offspring. She also is said to have laid in wait for people passing through her territory. She would then attack and devour them.

- **Ladon:** This son was a hundred-headed dragon. He lived with his sisters in the Garden of the Hesperides and was the prime guardian of the golden apples. After he is killed, he is turned into a great constellation of stars.

- **The Hesperides:** These daughters were nymphs. Their number varies from myth to myth (as do their parents), but most often they were known as three: Aegle, Erytheia, and Hesperethusa. The Hesperides were quite a bit better-looking than their sisters and they each had the gift of song. They lived in the Garden of the Hesperides and protected a tree with golden apples that grew there.

EURYBIA: MOTHER OF TITANS

Eurybia isn't quite as popular as her sister Ceto. Most myths involving Eurybia simply mention her as the wife of Crius (a Titan) and mother of three Titan sons: Astraeus, Pallas, and Perses. Astraeus would later father the winds and the stars; Pallas would become the father of Victory, Valor, and Strength; Perses would later father Hecate, a triple goddess.

NEREUS: THE ORIGINAL SEA KING

Nereus was a marine deity and was sometimes known as the "Old Man of the Sea." Though Poseidon is most often thought of first as the god of the sea, Nereus had this title well before Poseidon was even born. He had the ability to shape-shift—to take on various forms in different places—and also had the gift of prophecy. He is best known for fathering the Nereids (sea goddesses).

SIMPLE THAUMAS, BORN TO PROCREATE

Thaumas, also a sea deity, does not have a myth all to himself. He simply stood on the sidelines and was known only for his siring ability. He married Electra (an ocean deity) and fathered Iris and the Harpies. Iris was the personification of the rainbow as well as a messenger of the Olympian gods and goddesses. The Harpies were birdlike women who carried off the souls of the dead. They were also said to be responsible for anything that had gone missing, including children.

PHORCYS, FATHER TO THE SIRENS

Like his brothers, Phorcys was also a sea deity. However, he isn't often regarded for this attribute, but rather is best known for his offspring. As you know, Phorcys fathered several children by Ceto. However, some myths also claim that he was the father of the Sirens, which were sea deities: half woman, half bird. He is also rumored to be the father of Scylla, the famous sea monster.

Sea monster, from fifteenth- or sixteenth-century woodcuts

CYCLOPES AND THE HUNDRED-HANDED ONES

The Ugliest Siblings You'll Ever See

G

Gaia was quite the busy goddess. Not only did she give birth to three children on her own (Uranus, Pontus, and the Mountains), and bear five children (Ceto, Eurybia, Nereus, Thaumas, and Phorcys) with her son Pontus, she continued to give birth to a cacophony of mythological wonders. Here, we'll take a look at her multilimbed and one-eyed, wonderful children.

THE HUNDRED-HANDED ONES

In her work of creation, Gaia also mated with her other son, Uranus (Sky). The first children born to Gaia and Uranus were the Hecatoncheires, whose name means "Hundred-Handed Ones." There were three Hecatoncheires—named Cottus, Briareus (or Aegaeon), and Gyges (or Gyes)—and each had a hundred arms and fifty heads. These creatures are referred to as giants, although they differ from the giants of later myths.

The Hecatoncheires had incredible strength. For example, they could topple a mountain by bombarding it with boulders. Because of their outrageous strength, these creatures were feared—even by their own father, Uranus, ruler of the universe, who had them imprisoned in Tartarus (the Underworld).

Multitalented Monsters

The Cyclopes were a race of one-eyed giants. Sons of Gaia and Uranus, they were skilled craftsmen who designed the thunderbolt and gave it to Zeus as a weapon. In later myths, the Cyclopes are savage maneaters. The most famous was Polyphemos, son of Poseidon, who threatened Odysseus on his long journey home.

ONE-EYED WONDERS

Next, Gaia gave birth to three Cyclopes, also sired by Uranus. Like the Hecatoncheires, the Cyclopes also were giants in stature and possessed great strength and dexterity. The Cyclopes were ugly and frightening to look at; each had only one eye, centered in his forehead. You may think of the Cyclopes as fearsome, maneating monsters, and that is true in later myths. But these first Cyclopes, although bad-tempered, were not like that. Instead, they were known as the first smiths.

The three Cyclopes were considered storm deities: Brontes was known as Thunder or Thunderer; Arges was called the Shiner or Thunderbolt; and Steropes (sometimes Asteropes) had the nickname Lightning or Maker of Lightning. Uranus, fearing their strength, threw the Cyclopes into Tartarus, imprisoning them there with their brothers the Hecatoncheires.

MYTHS IN LITERATURE

Sources of Inspiration

G R

Myths tell such interesting and fundamental stories that it's no surprise that mythology has been a rich source of inspiration for authors. Its influence has been evident ever since the ancient Greeks and Romans began telling stories about the gods.

Authors work with mythology in many ways. Some refer to mythological characters or scenes to add flavor to their own works. Some writers will rework mythological styles or themes. Others use ancient myths as a starting point for their own stories. Now that you've begun to study classical mythology, you'll enjoy finding allusions to it in other books and stories.

Continue Your Research!

Because so many literary works refer to the ancient myths, this book can't cover them all. This section barely scratches the surface of the literature that's inspired by mythology. But don't let this stop you from exploring further!

Much literature of the medieval and Renaissance periods refers to classical mythology. For example, the medieval English poet Geoffrey Chaucer and the Renaissance playwright William Shakespeare both wrote versions of the tragic love story of Troilus and Cressida, set during the Trojan War. Shakespeare also wrote a poem titled *Venus and Adonis* in 1593. *The Divine Comedy,* written by Dante Alighieri between 1308 and 1321, is packed with classical allusions. For example, in *The Inferno*, the narrator's guide is Virgil, author of the *Aeneid*, and the poem is loaded with references to Apollo, Minerva (Athena), the Muses, and the hero Jason, to name just a few.

Later, John Milton adapted the form and themes of classical epic poetry to create his great poem *Paradise Lost* (1667). Although *Paradise Lost* is a Christian poem that tells the story of the fall of Adam and Eve, Milton admired classical poetry and used it to create a heroic Christian epic. Alexander Pope's poem *The Rape of the Lock* (1712) parodies classical conventions.

In the nineteenth century, classical mythology continued its influence on literature. Percy Bysshe Shelley's play *Prometheus Unbound* (1820) was inspired by a play of Aeschylus of the same name, but Shelley takes the story in a different direction to reflect the humanism of his own era. Shelley's wife Mary wrote the novel *Frankenstein* (1818), but did you know that her book's subtitle is *The Modern Prometheus*? The Romantic poet John Keats wrote poems such as "On First Looking into Chapman's Homer" (1816) and "Ode on a Grecian Urn" (1820), which deal with mythological themes. His well-known poem "Endymion" (1818) begins with the famous line "A thing of beauty is a joy for ever."

In the twentieth century, James Joyce's *Ulysses* (1922) used classical mythology in a new way. Joyce based the plot of his novel on the *Odyssey* (the Roman version of Odysseus's name is Ulysses), creating a modern story that parallels the characters and themes of the ancient epic. Although Ulysses is set in Dublin and takes place over the course of a single day instead of ten years, it patterns itself on the *Odyssey*. Although the characters have different names, they are reinterpretations of the main characters of the *Odyssey*. Joyce's novel is brilliant but difficult; a familiarity with classical mythology is essential to understand it.

Many contemporary authors have used classical mythology as a source for their stories. Here's a list of some recent novels inspired by the myths of ancient Greece and Rome:

- *The King Must Die* (1958) by Mary Renault. Read this novel for a retelling of the adventures of the young hero Theseus.
- *The Firebrand* (1987) by Marion Zimmer Bradley. The main character of this novel is Kassandra, daughter of Priam and unheeded prophetess, who recounts the story of the fall of Troy.
- *The Secret History* (1992) by Donna Tartt. This psychological thriller tells the story of a group of students fascinated by their Classics professor and the world of ancient Greece. Their re-enactment of the Dionysian rites leads to tragic results.
- *Troy* (2000) by Adèle Geras. This young adult novel (ages fourteen and older) imagines life inside Troy during the Trojan War.
- *Goddess of Yesterday: A Tale of Troy* (2002) by Caroline B. Cooney. Another young adult novel, written for readers ages twelve and up, this book retells the events leading up to the Trojan War from the perspective of Anaxandra, a young girl who comes to the court of Menelaus.
- *Last of the Amazons* (2002) by Steven Pressfield. The context for this novel is the conflict between the Amazons and Theseus, leader of the Athenians.
- *Ilium* (2003) and *Olympos* (2005) by Dan Simmons. If you like science fiction, take a look at these novels, which are packed with classical allusions and set the events of the *Iliad* and its aftermath on Mars and an alternate Earth.

- *The Songs of the Kings* (2004) by Barry Unsworth. This novel retells the story of Agamemnon's sacrifice of his daughter Iphigenia. Unsworth imaginatively probes ancient politics and heroes' desire to be immortalized in poetry.
- The *Troy* trilogy by David Gemmell. These three novels retell the story of the Trojan War, as familiar mythological characters interact with characters of the author's creation: *Lord of the Silver Bow* (2006), *Shield of Thunder* (2007), and *Fall of Kings* (2009, with Stella Gemmell).
- *Helen of Troy* (2006) by Margaret George. This novel imagines the story of Helen's life and the Trojan War from her own point of view.
- The *Cassandra Palmer* series by Karen Chance. This contemporary fantasy series, beginning with *Touch the Dark* (2006), is set amidst conflict between vampires and mages. Cassandra Palmer must learn to deal with the challenges and dangers of being Pythia, the world's foremost clairvoyant.
- *Lavinia* (2008) by Ursula K. LeGuin. This novel tells the story of the arrival of Aeneas and the Trojan refugees in Italy from the point of view of the Italian princess who will marry Aeneas.

Connecting Mythology to Modern Day

The Power of the Myth (1988), by Joseph Campbell with Bill Moyers, explores how mythology continues to affect people's everyday lives. Discussing everything from Darth Vader to marriage, this book is a must-read if you want to understand how mythology functions in the modern world.

THE TITANS AND TITANESSES

Get to Know the Original Twelve Gods

G

In Greek mythology, the deities formed and born at the beginning of the world weren't actually considered "gods" and "goddesses." They held power, but as the personification of an element or a division of the universe. When the Titans arrived, however, mythmakers began to describe them as gods and goddesses. The Titans and Titanesses were the "Original Twelve" in Greek mythology. So pay attention, and show some respect!

TITANIC OFFSPRING

You'd think after giving birth to Uranus (Sky), Pontus (Sea), and the Mountains (by herself); Ceto, Eurybia, Nereus, Thaumas, and Phorcys (with Pontus); and the Hundred-Handed Ones and the Cyclopes (with Uranus), Gaia might call it quits. (Indeed, mythmakers referred to her as "Mother Earth" for a reason.) However, Gaia wasn't finished: uniting again with her son Uranus, Gaia gave birth to the Titans and Titanesses.

These six sons of Gaia and Uranus were the Titans:

- **Coeus:** Not much is known about Coeus except that he was the father of Leto, who became the mother of Apollo and Artemis.
- **Crius:** He was the father of Astraeus, Pallas, and Perses.
- **Cronus:** The youngest Titan, Cronus overthrew his father in an epic struggle.

- **Hyperion:** The first god of the sun, Hyperion later sired Helios, who is the god most commonly associated with sun.
- **Iapetus:** Best known as the father of Prometheus, the champion of mankind, he also sired Epimetheus, Menoetius, and Atlas.
- **Oceanus:** The eldest of the Titans, Oceanus was the god of rivers.

These six daughters were the Titanesses:

- **Mnemosyne:** The personification of memory, she gave birth to the Muses.
- **Phoebe:** The first goddess of the moon, Phoebe was the mother of Leto.
- **Rhea:** A mother deity or earth goddess, Rhea was called the Mother of the Gods because she gave birth to the Olympians.
- **Tethys:** The first goddess of the sea, she gave birth to many children, including 3,000 daughters (yes, you read that right), called the Oceanids.
- **Theia:** This Titaness is best known for giving birth to Helios, Selene, and Eos.
- **Themis:** Goddess of necessity, Themis was the mother of Prometheus, the Hours, and (according to some myths) the Fates.

FAMILY FEUD:
URANUS OVERTHROWN

Uranus was afraid of his children, the Hecatoncheires and the Cyclopes, and imprisoned them in Tartarus. His relationship with the Titans was also one of fear and conflict.

Uranus loved ruling the universe and feared anything that threatened his power—and he viewed his children as such threats.

Therefore, he also decided to keep the Titans out of the way. Instead of imprisoning the Titans, however, Uranus tried to prevent them from being born by shoving each child back into Gaia's womb. He did this to all twelve of these children. Uranus, pleased with himself, was able to relax because he believed that his power was no longer threatened.

From Violence, New Life

Some myths state that the attack on Uranus caused the birth of other gods and goddesses. From the blood that soaked the ground, giants, nymphs, and the Furies sprang up. When Uranus's discarded genitals landed in the sea, great white foam arose. Aphrodite, goddess of love, was born of this foam and emerged from the sea fully grown.

Not surprisingly, Gaia was unhappy with the pain inflicted upon her and with her children's predicament. She decided to take action against Uranus. Gaia made a sharp sickle out of either iron or flint and complained to her children, suggesting they rise up and punish Uranus for his mistreatment of the whole family. Afraid of their father, the Titans and Titanesses refused their mother's request. Gaia, however, did not give up. She kept complaining and cajoling until Cronus, the youngest Titan, agreed to get revenge upon Uranus. Gaia smiled upon this favored son and told him her plan.

Cronus lay in wait that night, armed with the sickle his mother had made. Uranus began to make love to Gaia. Cronus, wasting no time, grabbed his father's genitals and sliced them off with the sickle. He tossed the severed organ from the heavens into the sea.

After this incident, Uranus seems to drop out of the picture. He was no longer worshiped or honored with sacrifice, and he held no power.

THE GIANTS

The Terrifying Race Only a Mother Could Love

G

Hera wasn't the only ancient deity to start a rebellion against Zeus, that brazen ruler of the heavens. Hera believed she could rule better than Zeus, and was severely punished for inciting rebellion (by being hung from the heavens with chains and anvils to weigh her down!). Despite this example, another deity plotted revenge against Zeus and the Olympians. Gaia (Mother Earth) was terribly upset that her children, the Titans, were imprisoned in Tartarus. So she rallied the Giants to avenge them, and battle her grandchildren, the Olympians.

The Giants were a very powerful race, with human heads and torsos but legs made of serpents. They were huge and had wild, thick hair and beards, and they terrified everything that crossed their paths.

The Giants represented a serious challenge to the Olympians. Aside from their colossal power and strength, the Giants could not be killed by an immortal alone. Instead, an immortal and a mortal had to work together to slay a Giant. To make matters even more difficult, some myths say that a certain plant could make the Giants immune to mortals' attacks. Zeus caught wind of this and had the plant removed from the Earth before the Giants could obtain it.

Ancient and Modern Interactions

Like many modern religions, classical mythology explores the relationship between humanity and a higher power. Myths often tell stories about direct interaction between people and the gods and goddesses. In classical mythology, those gods and goddesses often act based on emotion, not reason, which makes for some highly dramatic situations.

GIANTS VERSUS OLYMPIANS: A BATTLE OF THE AGES

The Giants initiated the battle by bombarding the heavens with boulders and flaming trees. Their actions certainly got the Olympians' attention. The gods quickly fought back, but because the Giants could not be killed, the Olympians struggled simply to hold their ground.

An oracle warned them that they needed the help of a mortal to win the war against the Giants. Zeus sent Athena to Earth to recruit Heracles, Zeus's son by a mortal woman. When Heracles entered the war, things started looking up for the Olympians. Athena and Heracles joined forces to bring down Alcyoneus, a leader of the Giants. While Athena attacked, Heracles shot the Giant with a poisoned arrow. Alcyoneus had special protection, however. He was immortal as long as he stood on his native soil. Therefore, Athena advised Heracles to drag the Giant outside of the boundaries of his land. Heracles did as he was told, and Alcyoneus died on the spot.

The next to fall was Alcyoneus's coleader, Porphyrion. Porphyrion attacked Hera, meaning to kill her. Instead, Zeus filled him with lust for her, turning the Giant's desire to kill into sexual passion. With Hera as the decoy, Zeus hurled a thunderbolt at Porphyrion, while Heracles shot him with an arrow. Porphyrion dropped dead, and Hera remained unharmed.

After the Giants' two leaders had fallen, an Olympian victory was assured. But the Giants did not give up easily. The Olympians had to combine their efforts and fight fiercely to win the war.

TYPHON

The Scariest Monster of Them All!

Greek mythology is full of fearsome, frightening creatures, and the great and powerful Typhon does not disappoint. Gaia, that life-giving deity with a take-no-prisoners attitude, created this terrifying creature after another familial upset. When Gaia learned the Olympians had defeated the Giants (in a fight to avenge the Titans' imprisonment in Tartarus), the situation looked bleak. Her sons were *still* locked up, and although it seemed they would remain there forever, Gaia had one last trick up her sleeve. She gave birth to a monster, Typhon. This creature was half man, half animal—and 100 percent terrifying.

Typhon had a hundred serpentine heads, each equipped with a flickering tongue and eyes that shot flames. Each head spoke with a different voice: human, god, beast, serpent, evil spirit, and more. Typhon had wings, his body was encircled with snakes, and he was almost incomprehensibly huge. When this creature spread his arms, one arm reached all the way to the west, and the other reached all the way to the east.

AND THE GODS SAID, "LET'S GET OUT OF HERE"

Typhon advanced toward Mount Olympus. At the sight of him, the gods and goddesses fled, transforming into various animals to disguise themselves. Aphrodite and Ares turned into fish, Apollo transformed into a bird, Hephaestus became an ox, Dionysus turned into a goat, and Hermes changed into an ibis. Only Zeus stood his ground against the fearsome enemy.

Athena's Bravery

You may be impressed by Zeus, the only god who remained in his original form in order to fight Typhon. However, some myths claim Athena also retained her own form, unfazed by the monstrous creature. In this version, Athena scolded Zeus for his cowardice; he had turned into a ram in order to avoid Typhon. As Athena stood bravely on Mount Olympus, Zeus returned to his real form, and the two faced Typhon together.

Zeus attacked Typhon with his mightiest weapon: the thunderbolt. By hurling thunderbolts continuously, so many they made the earth quake, Zeus pushed Typhon back a little. Thinking the monster was wounded, Zeus grabbed his sickle and left his fort, intending to finish him off. Typhon, however, wasn't as weak as Zeus thought, and a fierce fight ensued. Eventually, Typhon wrestled the sickle away from Zeus and used it to cut the tendons in his foe's arms and legs, leaving Zeus lying helpless on the ground. Typhon placed the tendons under the protection of the dragon Delphyne and carried Zeus off to a cave.

But all was not lost. Hermes and Pan joined forces to trick Delphyne. While the dragon was distracted, they stole the tendons and restored them to Zeus. Regaining his strength, Zeus immediately returned to Olympus, armed himself with thunderbolts, and went in search of Typhon.

AND THE BATTLE CONTINUES . . .

When Zeus caught up with Typhon, he showed the monster no mercy. Typhon tried to withstand the rain of thunderbolts, but he was no match for them. So he fled in hopes of finding a safe place where he could renew his strength. He encountered the Fates, who advised him he could be healed by eating the food the mortals ate. Typhon did as he was told, but the food of mortals only made him weaker.

Zeus caught up with Typhon and set loose another relentless shower of thunderbolts. Typhon tried hurling mountain peaks at Zeus, but the god used his thunderbolts to deflect them. The bloody battle continued until Typhon fled once more. According to one myth, Zeus picked up an island and flung it at Typhon. The island crushed the monster, trapping him. The myth states that because Typhon was immortal, he remains beneath the island—its volcanic eruptions are his fiery breath.

Another myth says that Zeus set Typhon on fire with the thunderbolts, seized the monster, and flung him into Tartarus, where he remains imprisoned with the Titans. Many say that Typhon is the cause of all dangerous winds—that's where the word *typhoon* came from.

Once again, Zeus was victorious in battle. After Zeus's defeat of Typhon, no one ever again challenged his right to rule gods and men. Thus the Olympians established their rule of the universe until the end of time.

CRONUS AND THE BIRTH OF ZEUS

G

Cronus defeated his father, Uranus, after Uranus tried to smother his children's strength. After Gaia gave birth to the Titans, power-hungry Uranus forced all the Titans and Titanesses back into their mother's womb, in order to prevent them from seizing control of the universe. In pain and unhappy, Gaia plotted with her children to overthrow their maniacal father. Cronus was the only Titan to agree with the plot, so he waited with a sickle inside his mother's womb, planning a violent sneak attack. When Uranus made love to Gaia, Cronus sliced off his genitals, and cast the severed organs into the sea. With the defeat of Uranus, the Titans, Titanesses, Cyclopes, and Hecatoncheires were all freed.

CRONUS CROWNED AS RULER

Cronus took his place as ruler of the universe and married his sister Rhea. Unfortunately, despite the injustice he'd suffered from Uranus, Cronus also fell victim to a lust for power.

No sooner had the Hecatoncheires and the Cyclopes been freed than they were once again imprisoned in Tartarus by Cronus. He feared these giants as his father had. However, he allowed his brothers and sisters, the Titans and Titanesses, to keep their freedom.

LIKE FATHER, LIKE SON

Cronus was every bit as power-hungry as his father had been. As a result, he was not a very good ruler and a terrible father. Cronus had heard a prophecy that one of his children would overthrow him. So he devised a scheme to prevent his own children from ever challenging him.

Cronus remembered that his mother had planned and initiated the overthrow of Uranus. But he also realized that Gaia probably wouldn't have called for this revenge if she had not been so burdened by the children in her womb. So Cronus decided to remove the threat of his children himself.

Every year for five years, Rhea gave birth to a child. As soon as the child left her womb, it went straight into the mouth of Cronus. Instead of trying to hold the children inside their mother's body, Cronus literally took them into his own by swallowing them whole.

Rhea was overcome with grief and rage. She couldn't stand to have her children taken away from her so soon after their birth. Cronus had underestimated a mother's love for her children and her natural instinct to protect them. Rhea's maternal feelings became the driving force behind her own scheme of revenge.

When Rhea conceived her sixth child, she asked her mother for help. Gaia sent her to the island of Crete, where she gave birth to Zeus. Rhea returned to Cronus after the child was born but left Zeus behind. She tricked her husband by wrapping a large stone in swaddling cloths and telling Cronus it was Zeus. Cronus swallowed the stone, believing it was his sixth child. Meanwhile, the real Zeus remained unharmed.

ZEUS VERSUS CRONUS: THE BATTLE WITH THE TITANS

Don't Mess with Zeus (Or, Always Listen to Prometheus)

G

When Cronus took over the universe from Uranus, he quickly became as power-hungry as his father was. Heeding the prophecy he heard that his children would overthrow him, Cronus decided to prevent them from growing up in the first place. Whenever a new child was born to Rhea, Cronus would swallow them whole. Furious and heartbroken, Rhea decided to hide her sixth child, Zeus, with his grandmother Gaia. She wrapped a rock in baby's clothing, and Cronus gulped it down, thinking it was his child. Zeus, therefore, survived in secret.

AN INCREDIBLE CHILDHOOD

Zeus was left in the care of Gaia. The Curetes (minor gods) and the Nymphs (nature goddesses) helped care for the infant. The Curetes would mimic the rituals of the Cretan youths by performing dances and clashing their weapons together. Their racket hid the cries of the baby Zeus so his father would not discover him.

Like any other baby, Zeus needed nourishment. The nymph Amalthea was responsible for feeding Zeus and suckled him through his infancy.

Thank Your Lucky Stars

Some myths say that Amalthea was a she-goat and that Zeus was extremely grateful to her. When Amalthea died, Zeus showed his appreciation by turning Amalthea into the constellation known as Capricorn (the goat). He also used her skin to create a shield that he carried into battle.

Zeus was well cared for as he grew into adulthood. A strong, healthy young man, Zeus prepared to fulfill the prophecy and overthrow his father. He left Crete and visited his cousin, Metis, an Oceanid who was the daughter of Tethys and Oceanus. Metis, well known for her wisdom, agreed to help Zeus. She advised him to become a servant of Cronus and, in that position, to place a potion in his drink. Zeus did as he was told. The potion caused Cronus to vomit—and out came Zeus's brothers and sisters, whole and unharmed.

AT WAR WITH THE TITANS

With his rescued siblings, Zeus had the beginnings of an army with which to challenge Cronus. However, Cronus had some difficulty in assembling his own forces. Some of the Titans refused to help him in the struggle. None of the Titanesses participated, and Oceanus, Cronus's brother, also refused to fight. Similarly, Helios, son of Hyperion, refused to take part in the war. Prometheus and Epimetheus, sons of Iapetus, blatantly refused to pledge loyalty to Cronus; rather, they eventually sided with Zeus's army. The remaining Titans chose Atlas, another son of Iapetus, to lead them into battle.

In preparation for war, each side created fortifications. Led by Atlas, the Titans gathered at Mount Othrys; the children of Cronus, under Zeus, gathered at Mount Olympus.

The war was a monumental conflict. The Titans were awesome creatures who possessed considerable strength. The children of Cronus were just as strong and cunning. The two sides met on the battlefield every day for ten long years, each side winning some battles and losing others. After ten years, however, the war was no closer to a decisive victory. So Gaia, who knew a thing or two about overthrowing one's father, interceded and advised Zeus.

Gaia told Zeus that freeing the Cyclopes and Hecatoncheires from Tartarus would gain the Olympians some very powerful allies. Zeus wasted no time. He ventured into the depths of the Underworld and faced Campe, a monster appointed by Cronus to guard the giants. Zeus slew Campe and freed his uncles. As Gaia had predicted, the Hecatoncheires and the Cyclopes were so angry with Cronus for his treatment of them that they joined forces with the Olympians.

With these giants newly recruited to Zeus's army, the tide of the war began to turn. The Cyclopes built impressive weapons, including lightning, thunder, earthquake, a trident, and a helmet of invisibility. The Hecatoncheires threw great boulders at the Titans' fort, weakening it.

Atlas's Punishment

Atlas, leader of the Titans' army, escaped imprisonment in Tartarus—only to find himself suffering an even greater punishment. Zeus decreed that Atlas must hold the weight of the sky and heavens upon his shoulders for eternity.

Zeus laid siege to Mount Othrys. But strength alone would not win the war, so he devised a plan to force Cronus's army to surrender. Using the helmet of invisibility, one of the Olympians walked into the camp unnoticed and stole all of Cronus's weapons. Another Olympian distracted Cronus with the trident while Zeus shot lightning bolts. Meanwhile, the Cyclopes and Hecatoncheires rained boulders down upon the Titans. Zeus's strategy succeeded, and the war that had nearly destroyed the universe was finally over.

ZEUS IN CHARGE

When Zeus became the new ruler, his first task was to dispose of his enemies. The army of Cronus was imprisoned in Tartarus with the Hecatoncheires standing guard to ensure they would not escape.

Zeus was harsh in punishing his enemies and generous in rewarding his allies. The Titanesses, who did not participate in the war, were allowed to retain their power and their positions in the heavens. Zeus also restored the powers of any immortal who had supported him and had been dispossessed by Cronus. And of course, his brothers and sisters received their own rights and powers. The reign of the Olympians began.

MOUNT OLYMPUS AND MYTHOLOGICAL LAWS

The Home of the Gods, a Center for Law and Order

G

Mount Olympus, home to the Olympian gods and goddesses, is described only vaguely in classical mythology. Some myths state that it was a mountain higher than any other on Earth. In these accounts, Mount Olympus has several peaks, each home to a different deity, with Zeus residing on the topmost peak. Other myths refer to Mount Olympus as part of the heavens and not on Earth at all.

Regardless of its exact location, Mount Olympus was a magnificent place, clearly fit for the gods. Beyond the entranceway of clouds were several luxurious palaces and halls, built by Hephaestus, where the Olympians lived and held parties.

For the most part, life on Mount Olympus was easy and peaceful. The gods and goddesses lounged around, feasting on ambrosia and drinking nectar while listening to music and watching graceful dances. Mount Olympus was untouched by the natural disasters and inconveniences that afflicted Earth, such as thunderstorms, snow, rough winds, earthquakes, hailstorms, and tornadoes. The atmosphere was one of pleasure and peace, making the inhabitants peaceful (well, most of the time).

Mount Olympus was more than the dwelling place of the gods and goddesses. It was also their command center, the place where trials were held, laws were created, and important decisions were made.

ZEUS THE SUPREME RULER

As ruler of gods and men, Zeus had the duty of bringing ulti-mate order to the universe. An order of sorts had already been established—the universe had come a long way from the chaos that had preceded it—but Zeus wanted to refine this order further.

Zeus made love to his aunt, Themis, who was the goddess of eternal order. Their union produced numerous daughters, including six who became the personifications of the principles needed to complete the ultimate order he desired. These daughters of Zeus and Themis were:

- **Eirene:** The personification of peace
- **Eunomia:** The personification of law and order
- **Dike:** The personification of justice
- **Clotho:** The Fate who was responsible for spinning the thread of life
- **Lachesis:** The Fate who was responsible for measuring the thread of life
- **Atropos:** The Fate who was responsible for cutting the thread of life

With universal order now established, it became Zeus's job to maintain that order, and he was fully capable of doing so. Zeus was known as a strict but fair ruler who firmly believed in justice.

Zeus did not allow his emotions or biases to affect his rule. If he felt he could not judge a matter impartially, he would either bring it before a council of other deities or find some other way (such as a contest) to determine the final outcome. For example, Zeus's brother Poseidon had a tendency to fight for land and often started battles with other gods and goddesses. Sometimes Zeus thought he could not decide impartially between his brother and, say, his daughter. Who would want to make such a choice? So Zeus would bring the matter before the council or create a contest whose winner could rightfully claim the land. Occasionally Zeus also used compromise to settle a dispute.

In matters of law, Zeus could be very wise. He did have his weaknesses, though—especially women. And some myths say that even though Zeus was supreme ruler, he did not have complete control. Remember his daughters the Fates? All of the gods—even the great Zeus himself—were subject to these three personifications of destiny.

SOWING THE SEEDS OF MUTINY

You might think that the beauty, tranquility, and splendor of Mount Olympus would be enough to keep the peace. With the ascendancy of the Olympians, law and order were set, justice usually prevailed, and the universe was ruled with intelligence instead of by brute force. Despite this near-utopia, a rebellion was brewing among the gods—one that would threaten the power of Zeus.

THE GODS REBEL!

The rebellion on Mount Olympus began with three key figures: Athena, Hera, and Poseidon. (Several myths show Hera as the mastermind behind the scheme.) Each of these gods felt that he or she could rule better than Zeus, so they banded together to rally the other gods and goddesses against him. Except for Hestia, all of the other gods joined them.

As Zeus lay sleeping, the group chained him to his bed. They set his weapons out of reach and then congratulated each other on an easy and successful coup. However, their celebration was short-lived. Now that Zeus had been overwhelmed, who would take his place?

The Olympians began to argue, each convinced that he or she would make the best supreme ruler. Not one of the powerful deities was willing to back down. The argument continued for a long time, growing more heated as levels of frustration rose.

Trouble with Hera

Hera's punishment is recorded in mythology, but some myths say that the ordeal was punishment for a different infraction. These myths record that Zeus punished his wife in this manner because of her relentless and overzealous persecution of his son Heracles.

While the deities were preoccupied with their claims to power, Thetis, a sea goddess, came to Zeus's rescue. She ventured down to Tartarus and appealed to Briareus (one of the Hecatoncheires) for help; he consented and unchained Zeus. As you might imagine, Zeus was furious at the Olympians' actions. With Zeus free, they quickly backed down, not daring to challenge him face to face. Zeus reclaimed his position as supreme ruler and forced all Olympians to vow that they would never again challenge his power.

PUNISHING HERA

Zeus, as lord of justice (and also out of revenge), decided to punish Hera for her insubordination. He had her suspended from the heavens by attaching chains to her wrists and anvils to her feet to weigh her down. After her eventual release, Hera never incited another rebellion.

THE TWELVE OLYMPIAN GODS

The World's First Celebrities

Ⓖ

From the creation of the world from Chaos, to the battle between Cronus and Zeus, the heavens faced serious tumult. After Cronus was defeated, however, this family conflict ended. The children of Cronus united, dividing their realm among them. They agreed, however, that they needed a supreme ruler, and unanimously chose Zeus. Here we'll introduce the twelve main Olympian gods and goddesses—some of the most famous and powerful deities in Greek mythology.

THREE BROTHERS, THREE DOMINIONS

After the fall of Cronus, his three sons—Zeus, Poseidon, and Hades—divided the dominions. (To be fair, they drew lots.) The three realms up for grabs were the heavens, the seas, and the land of the dead. (Mount Olympus would remain the realm of all the gods, with no one god having control.)

Zeus drew the heavens, which made him the ruler of the gods and the heavens both. Depictions of Zeus often show him as wearing a helmet, wielding one of his thunderbolts, and protected by the aegis (a breastplate or shield). He is also often accompanied by an eagle, an attendant that symbolizes his power.

Poseidon drew the seas as his realm. In the myths, Poseidon often appears as a violent god, associated with savage sea storms and earthquakes. He is depicted as tall with a long, flowing beard, and wielding his trident, which was one of the weapons made by the Cyclopes during the war against Cronus. He may be pictured with seashells or various kinds of sea creatures. Poseidon was also associated with horses; the ancients imagined rearing horses in the mighty waves that crashed into the shore.

The third brother, Hades, drew the Underworld, land of the dead. The Greek Underworld is not the same as the Christian concept of hell, nor was Hades considered evil or satanic. In Greek mythology, Hades appears as a loner uninterested in the world of the living. He is often depicted holding a key, signifying his status as the god who keeps the dead locked away from the world of the living. Like Poseidon, Hades was associated with horses; some myths say that Hades, not Poseidon, created the horse.

THREE SISTERS: THE GREATEST GODDESSES

Zeus's sisters did not participate in the drawing of lots, but they had their own powers. The realms governed by Hera, Hestia, and Demeter were essential to an orderly universe.

Hera was the greatest of the Greek goddesses. As Zeus's sister and wife, she was queen of the heavens. Jealous and vindictive, Hera possessed both a quick temper and fearsome passion. She was the protector of wives, defender of marriage, and a goddess of childbirth. Her depictions emphasize her queenly stature: She appears as tall and stately, wielding a scepter. Her bird was the peacock.

Hestia, goddess of hearth and home, does not appear in many surviving myths. Despite this, she is thought to have been held sacred and worshiped in every ancient household. Hestia was closely associated with virginity.

Demeter's name means "Mother Earth." Don't confuse her with Gaia, however. Gaia was Earth itself. Her granddaughter Demeter had dominion over the fruits of the Earth, the power of fertility, and agriculture. Demeter loved to be close to the soil. Whereas her sister Hestia never left Mount Olympus, Demeter rarely stayed there, preferring to spend time on Earth. Demeter is often shown seated and may be depicted with a torch or sheaves of grain. Her bird was the crane, her animal the serpent.

SIX MORE GODS TO LOVE

The previous six gods and goddesses were the original Olympians, but they were only half the story. There were twelve great Olympians in all, each playing an important role in the order of the universe. There is some disagreement about which gods make up the final six; following are the top eight contenders.

Athena

As the goddess of wisdom, Athena was held in high regard by mortal and immortal alike. She was also the goddess of war, crafts, and skills. Unlike Ares, however, Athena was not bloodthirsty. She preferred peace to war. Even so, when she was involved in battle, she proved herself to be an invincible strategist, dominating the field.

Athena usually appears dressed in armor, helmet, and aegis. She wields a spear and a shield. She is associated with the owl (which symbolizes wisdom), and an owl often perches on her shoulder.

What on Earth Is an Aegis?

The aegis, Athena's shield or breastplate, was said to have been made by Hephaestus, the Olympians' smith. Hephaestus incorporated the severed head of the Gorgon Medusa into the aegis. Because Medusa's frightful appearance could turn men to stone, the aegis was an effective weapon that paralyzed enemies with fear. The word *aegis* has made its way into the English language; it means "protection" or "support."

Ares

Ares, god of war, lived for battle and bloodshed, deriving great pleasure from human warfare. Ares appears in many poems and myths and was worshiped in Sparta, particularly before a battle was to take place.

Depictions of Ares show him wearing armor and a helmet and carrying a spear, sword, and shield. He was associated with the dog and the vulture. Although he was the war god, Ares was not always victorious. In fact, he was defeated in battle several times throughout the myths.

Artemis

As goddess of the hunt, Artemis had little interest in anything besides the thrill of the chase. She roamed the mountains with a band of nymphs, expertly hunting animals (and sometimes men). Although her primary activity was hunting, Artemis was also the protector of children, wild animals, and the weak. Legend has it that her arrows could cause sudden death without pain. You wouldn't want to get on her bad side, though—Artemis could be a vindictive and vengeful goddess.

Leto's Protectors

If Hera had had her way, Artemis and her brother Apollo would never have been born. When Zeus had an affair with Leto, Hera was determined that the union would produce no children. But Leto escaped Hera and gave birth, first to Artemis. The newborn Artemis helped her mother through nine days of intensive labor, which ended with the birth of Apollo. Because their mother had suffered so much for them, Artemis and Apollo became her fierce protectors.

Artemis is usually depicted carrying her weapon of choice: a bow and arrows. Some myths describe her as a girl-child—a virgin with eternal youth—who was as wild as the animals she both hunted and protected. As all wild animals were within her domain, she was not associated with one animal in particular, although she often appears with a stag or a hunting dog.

Apollo

Apollo, Artemis's twin brother, was the god of archery, music, and poetry. While his sister lived only for the hunt, Apollo was a versatile god who enjoyed a great many things. At times, he was a shepherd or a cowherd; at other times he was a great musician. Apollo was also important to prophecy and medicine. He had the ability to inflict illness as well as to cure it.

Because Apollo dabbled in so many arts, there isn't a single typical depiction of him. You might see him playing his lyre, shooting an arrow, or driving a chariot. One constant in all depictions of Apollo, though, is his great beauty, which was considered ideal. Apollo was associated with several different animals—including the wolf, deer, dolphin, crow, vulture, and swan—and he was also associated with the laurel tree.

Hermes

Hermes was the god of commerce, travel, and athletics. He brought luck to people, guided travelers and merchants, and protected rogues and thieves. Hermes was an active god, renowned for his agility and athleticism. He was one of the few gods who could enter the Underworld and leave it again without deterrence. He's probably best known, however, as the messenger of the gods.

Hermes is normally shown wearing a winged hat and winged sandals, which symbolize his swiftness (a good trait in a messenger). He is also sometimes shown carrying either a golden herald's wand or a staff with two serpents' heads. Hermes was a trickster who could be mischievous but who also had a kind heart.

Aphrodite

Nearly everyone has heard of Aphrodite—the goddess of love. (You may know her as Venus, which was her Roman name.) Some myths present Aphrodite as a flaky, somewhat ridiculous character; others describe her as a generous and benevolent goddess, due the same reverence as the other Olympians. Regardless of her character, Aphrodite was always passionate.

Aphrodite was a great beauty, with a sweet and seductive smile. Her myths almost always involve love affairs: Either she's having affairs of her own, or she's meddling in those of others. This goddess was associated with the dove, and her plants were the rose and myrtle.

Hephaestus

Hephaestus was Aphrodite's husband. You might assume that the goddess of love would be married to a handsome, charming husband. But that wasn't the case among the Olympians. In fact,

Hephaestus, son of Zeus and Hera, was thrown out of heaven at his birth because of his ugliness and deformities.

As the god of fire, smithing, craftsmanship, and metalworking, Hephaestus erected great palaces for the gods and goddesses and made armor for those he favored. A skilled craftsman, he could build just about anything. Hephaestus is associated with volcanoes, which were thought to be his workshops.

Hephasteus's Misfortunes

Some myths state that Hephaestus was born healthy, without any deformities. In this version of his story, Hephaestus took Hera's side in an argument with Zeus. In anger, Zeus threw the god from the heavens, and Hephaestus fell for nine days and nine nights before he landed on an island. His not-so-gentle landing made him lame.

Dionysus

Dionysus was the god of the vine, wine, and revelry. Whereas most of the Olympians snubbed mortals, Dionysus mingled directly with his mortal followers. His religious festivals often turned into rites of ecstasy.

Dionysus's greatest gift to humanity was the gift of wine, which could provide relief from a person's burdens, if only for a while. However, Dionysus was sometimes cruel—as all gods could be. Those who opposed him felt his wrath. Dionysus is most often associated with grapevines, dance, music, wine, madness, and sex.

ZEUS AND HERA

The Royal Family with Commitment Issues

G

In the ancient world, Zeus was known as a womanizer. He had several love affairs after gaining power as supreme ruler, but after all of these love affairs ended, Zeus set his sights on his sister Hera. Zeus believed that only this goddess could match him well enough in power to become his permanent wife. Zeus was so used to getting what he wanted that it never occurred to him that he might not be able to have Hera. By nature, Hera was highly jealous. She knew about Zeus's past loves and wasn't too keen on his advances. So Zeus had to trick Hera into becoming his wife.

Zeus disguised himself as a cuckoo and created a great rainstorm. In the guise of the cuckoo, he took advantage of Hera's sympathy. Feeling sorry for the poor, drenched bird, Hera picked it up and folded it inside her clothes, clutching it to her body. Zeus transformed back into his own form and violated Hera. Dishonored and shamed, Hera agreed to become his wife.

Secret Lovers

Some myths state that this wasn't the first time Zeus and Hera were together. They had several secret rendezvous before the war with the Titans. This version of their story may explain Hera's jealousy and resentment toward Zeus's other lovers.

A WEDDING FIT FOR THE GODS

The marriage ceremony between Zeus and Hera was a grand affair. Different myths give different locations for the divine wedding:

- The *Iliad* places the ceremony on the peak of Mount Ida in Phrygia.
- Other sources say the wedding took place in Euboea, the place where the deities came to rest after returning from the island of Crete.
- Still other sources say that Zeus and Hera were married in the Garden of the Hesperides, located in the westernmost part of the world.

Wherever it took place, the wedding was a magnificent party attended by all of the gods and goddesses. Even Hades left his dark realm to witness the marriage of his brother and sister. The myths say that the tradition of bringing gifts to a newly married couple began with Zeus and Hera. Gaia gave Hera a splendid tree that bore golden apples. This tree was planted in the Garden of the Hesperides and protected by the nymphs.

This divine ceremony became the standard for sacred marriage throughout Greece. Festivals were held to honor the sanctity of marriage and to commemorate the union of Zeus and Hera. In Athens, it became a tradition for brides to receive apples and pomegranates, the favorite fruits of Hera. Throughout Greece, wedding ceremonies were preceded by a procession in which a statue of Hera dressed as a bride was wheeled through the town. Sometimes the statue was wheeled right to the marriage bed. Also, the month attributed to Hera became the traditional time for weddings. (What month was that? Here's a hint: Hera's Roman name is Juno.) Hera became the goddess of marriage, protecting wives and punishing adulterers.

THE CHILDREN OF ZEUS AND HERA

Some myths say that the wedding night of Zeus and Hera lasted for 300 years! Despite their extended honeymoon, the couple had only three children—together, that is.

Ares

According to most myths, Ares was the only son of Zeus and Hera. Ares would become the god of war, taking his place among the great gods of Olympus.

Eileithyia

Some myths imply that Eileithyia was born out of wedlock. In any case, this daughter of Zeus and Hera was the goddess of childbirth. Hera sometimes took advantage of her daughter's role as the helper of women during labor, and Eileithyia rarely questioned her mother's wishes. For example, jealous Hera wanted to prevent Leto from giving birth to Zeus's children, so she tried to prevent Eileithyia from going to Leto's side. Eileithyia wanted to obey her mother, but other goddesses convinced her to help Leto. When Eileithyia arrived there, Artemis was born.

Another example involved the birth of Heracles. Again, Hera's jealousy was intense. She told Eileithyia to sit outside the room where Heracles's mother (Alcmene, a mortal lover of Zeus) was in labor, keeping her own arms, legs, and fingers crossed (or simply clutching her own knees together). This action postponed the birth of Heracles for several days.

Outsmarting Eileithyia

Heracles was born thanks to the clever servant who attended Alcmene during her labor. Although Alcmene's child had not been born yet, the servant pretended that he had, shouting, "It's a boy!" Eileithyia, shocked that her spell had failed, got up and went to see the child. When she uncrossed her limbs, the spell was broken, and Alcmene was able to give birth.

Hebe

Hebe was less prominent than her brother and sister, but she was known for her beauty. The personification of youth, Hebe was forever young and beautiful. She was cupbearer to the Olympians, serving them their divine drink of nectar. Hebe also drew baths, helped Hera into her chariot, and took care of other household chores.

One myth says that Hebe was released from her cupbearing duties when she accidentally tripped and fell at an important festival. As she fell, she indecently exposed herself to the guests and, as a result, lost her job of serving. Later, however, Hebe became the bride of Heracles when he was admitted into the heavens.

Hephaestus: A Fourth Child?

Some myths state that Zeus and Hera had a fourth child together. In those versions, Hephaestus was their second son. But Hesiod tells the story a different way, claiming that Hera conceived Hephaestus without the aid of Zeus or any other man. In this popular version of the myth, Zeus and Hera argue, and afterward Hera gives birth to Hephaestus by an act of sheer will.

POSEIDON

An Ancient Schoolyard Bully—But Much More Dangerous

G

Often considered second in command to Zeus, Poseidon was the powerful god of the sea, a god who garnered more fear than respect. He controlled the seas and could create earthquakes. Sailors tried to placate Poseidon, but most of the ancients regarded him as a god best avoided.

POSEIDON'S REALMS

When the Olympian gods divided the domains by drawing lots, Poseidon drew the seas. However, his power extended beyond the sea to include other bodies of water, such as lakes and freshwater springs. Some myths say he also controlled the rivers, although most rivers had their own lesser deities.

Poseidon was often called "Earth-Shaker" because he had the power to create earthquakes. Using his trident, he could generate savage sea storms, force the waves as high as he desired, summon sea monsters, and cause landslides and floods. He answered to no one except Zeus, and even Zeus could not always rein him in before severe damage was done. It is no wonder Poseidon was feared by all, especially seafarers.

But even with the power of the seas at his command, Poseidon was not satisfied with his realm. He wanted more; Poseidon was one of the original three Olympians who conspired against Zeus, wanting to take over his role as ruler of the gods. When the attempted mutiny failed, the sea god tried to heighten his standing by becoming the patron of more cities than the other gods.

THE FIGHT FOR ATHENS

Poseidon came into conflict with Athena over the city of Athens. Even before this happened, Poseidon bore several grudges against his niece. Poseidon was considered the least clever of the Olympian gods, and Athena was the goddess of wisdom. He was the god of the sea and wanted the ocean reserved for his creatures alone. When Athena taught mortals the art of shipbuilding, she opened up Poseidon's domain to humans. Remember, too, that some myths credit Poseidon with creating the horse, a wild and beautiful beast. Athena gave the bridle to mortals, enabling people to tame Poseidon's creation and use it for their own purposes. So a good deal of animosity already existed between the two deities—and this was heightened when each claimed the city of Athens.

One myth states that Zeus allowed the people of Athens to choose their deity by deciding which of the two gifts was more useful. The people judged that the olive tree was more useful than a saltwater spring, so Athena became protector of the city.

FIGHTING FOR CONTROL

Poseidon didn't give up easily. He continued to challenge the gods and goddesses for the patronage of other cities. Numerous disputes took place, and more often than not Poseidon was the loser. Here are some of the better-known conflicts:

- He challenged Dionysus for the island of Naxos and lost.
- He wanted Delphi but had to go up against Apollo, who won.
- He competed again with Athena for Troezen, and lost.
- He challenged Zeus for Aegina. Zeus, of course, won.
- He challenged Hera for the city of Argos, but the Queen of the Heavens won.

Despite these setbacks, many cities honored Poseidon as their chief god—including Corinth, Helike, and Aegae—and representatives of the twelve cities of the Ionian League met every year at a temple of Poseidon.

POSEIDON'S QUEEN

Amphitrite was the daughter of Nereus (the Old Man of the Sea) and Doris (a daughter of Oceanus). She was part of a circle of deities called the Nereids, who were sea nymphs said to be the personification of the waves. Some myths say there were one hundred Nereids; others claim there were only fifty. Regardless, Amphitrite stood apart from her many sisters in one respect: She was the leader of their chorus.

One day, Amphitrite and her sisters were dancing and singing on the island of Naxos. Poseidon noticed her and fell in love. He carried Amphitrite off to be his bride. Other myths argue that Amphitrite did not give in so easily.

Although Poseidon ruled the seas, Amphitrite wasn't impressed by her suitor. Her father was the Old Man of the Sea, a deity who'd been in power long before Poseidon. But Poseidon claimed to love her, and he was unaccustomed to being refused. Amphitrite wanted nothing to do with Poseidon and tried to escape to the deepest parts of the ocean, but Poseidon always found her. A band of dolphins captured Amphitrite and handed her over to Poseidon. She finally agreed to be his wife. Amphitrite bore Poseidon three children: Benthesicyme, Rhode, and Triton.

POSEIDON'S LOVERS AND THEIR CHILDREN

Much like his brother Zeus, Poseidon had many affairs. Unlike Hera, however, Poseidon's wife was neither jealous nor vindictive. Poseidon had affairs with mortals and immortals alike, fathering many children. Many of his conquests include:

- **Aethra**, daughter of the king of Troezen. The night Poseidon and Aethra made love, Aethra had also made love with Aegeus, the ruler of Athens. Aethra conceived a child that night—but no one knew whether the father was Aegeus or Poseidon. Most believed that the child was Poseidon's, although Aegeus claimed the child, a son, as his own. The child, Theseus, became a famous hero.
- **Amymone**, one of the fifty daughters of King Danaus. Poseidon made love to Amymone while she was searching for water in the land of Argos. He had stopped a satyr from raping Amymone, then proceeded to court Amymone for himself. After making love to her, Poseidon used his trident to create a spring so Amymone could bring water back to her family. Amymone and Poseidon had a son from their union: Nauplius, whose extensive knowledge of the seas and astronomy would make him a hero to seafarers.
- **Demeter**, Poseidon's sister. Wishing to escape her brother's advances, Demeter transformed herself into a mare. But Poseidon

wasn't to be put off. He transformed himself into a stallion and mated with her in a pasture, both of them in the form of horses. Together they produced Desponia, a nymph, and Arion, a wild horse.

- **Iphimedia**, an unhappily married woman, was in love with Poseidon and made a habit of walking along the seashore. She would often sit down and scoop up the water, allowing it to flow over her breasts. Poseidon found this alluring, and his union with Iphimedia produced two sons: the Giants Ephialtes and Otus.

- **Medusa**, a Gorgon with snakes for hair and a terrifying appearance that could turn anyone to stone. Some myths say, however, that Medusa wasn't always this fearsome creature; she was once a beautiful woman, and her beauty caught Poseidon's eye. Poseidon and Medusa made love in one of Athena's temples—an act unacceptable to the virgin goddess Athena. As punishment, Athena turned Medusa into the horrifying creature she is known as today. She also helped Perseus to slay Medusa. When Perseus cut off Medusa's head, two children appeared—Chrysaor and Pegasus—the results of her union with Poseidon.

- **Theophane**, a beautiful young woman who had several suitors, including Poseidon. To avoid competition, Poseidon abducted Theophane and took her to an island. Theophane's suitors searched for their missing love, but before they could reach her Poseidon turned the island's inhabitants to sheep—including Theophane. Poseidon transformed himself into a ram. When the suitors arrived, Poseidon changed the sheep into wolves that slaughtered the suitors instead. Poseidon and Theophane mated while in their sheep forms, so their son (whose name is not recorded) was born a ram with a fleece of gold and the ability to speak and fly.

- **Thoosa**, the daughter of Phorcys (a son of Gaia). Her affair with Poseidon is known mostly for its offspring: the Cyclops

Polyphemus. Polyphemus was not from the original Cyclopes race. Instead, he was a violent, savage, maneating creature.

POSEIDON AND THE TROJANS

Any overview of Poseidon must mention his relationship with the Trojans, a relationship that's central to understanding this god. As punishment for their participation in the uprising against Zeus, Poseidon and Apollo were forced to help Laomedon, the king of Troy, build walls around his city. They were to be compensated for this great work, but when it came time to pay, Laomedon refused, angering both gods. Apollo inflicted a great plague on the city and was satisfied with this revenge. Poseidon sent a sea monster to harass Troy, but his anger continued.

Later, during the Trojan War, Poseidon sided with the Greeks—despite Zeus's order to stay out of the conflict. Because of his anger and bitterness, Poseidon made life hard for everyone during the Trojan War.

WORSHIPING POSEIDON

Poseidon was widely worshiped throughout ancient Greece. Sailors offered sacrifices to Poseidon in hopes of calm seas, and he was also connected with fresh water and fertility. Yet he was greatly feared for his ability to whip up storms and cause earthquakes, as well as for his unpredictable nature.

HADES

The Fearsome Lord of the Underworld

G

In the ancient world, death was just as complicated as life. The Underworld was the place where all souls (or "shades" as they were often called) went after death. Hades, a private god, was the ruler of the Underworld, and this dark and mysterious deity was feared as much as he was respected.

When the Olympian brothers drew lots for their domains, Hades drew the realm of the dead. This kingdom suited him very well. Hades was a somber, grim god who enjoyed solitude. Although the ancients often described Hades as cold, he was never associated with evil. He was simply the ruler of the dead, and he performed his duties efficiently and with an unrelenting sense of responsibility. Hades never allowed pity—or any emotion, for that matter—to interfere with his work.

Hades was one of the six original Olympians. But he rarely visited Mount Olympus and didn't socialize with the other gods, so he was effectively kicked out of the top twelve. (This suited Hades just fine, because he had no desire to take part in divine councils.) In his own realm, Hades reigned supreme; most gods stayed away from the Underworld. There, Hades had complete control, and even Zeus usually left him alone.

HADES AND PERSEPHONE: FORCED LOVE

Although Hades rarely left his realm to visit the land of the living, the myths say he visited the mortal world at least once. During this visit, he encountered the beautiful Persephone, daughter of Demeter and Zeus.

Hades noticed Persephone as she gathered flowers on a plain in Sicily, accompanied by some nymphs. He was immediately overwhelmed by her beauty and didn't bother to court her. Instead, he abducted her and took her to the Underworld.

Persephone was a prisoner in Hades's realm. Her mother, Demeter, was frantic at the sudden disappearance of her daughter, and she traveled the world searching for her.

Dire Consequences

Demeter was an earth goddess and as she searched, crops failed, causing people to suffer and go hungry. This was when the first winter came to the world. Because of Demeter's great sorrow and the starving people's cries, Zeus refused to allow a marriage between Hades and Persephone.

Zeus sent Hermes to persuade Hades to release Persephone. Hades couldn't bear the thought of giving up Persephone, but the message brought by Hermes was a direct order from Zeus. Hades had little choice but to let the girl go. Before he did, however, he found a loophole.

Hades pretended to comply with Zeus's orders while he created a plan to keep Persephone. According to a law of the all-powerful Fates, anyone who ate food in the Underworld could never return to the land of the living. Knowing this law, Hades tricked Persephone into eating some pomegranate seeds. (The number of seeds varies according to individual myths: either four, seven, or eight.) Because Persephone ate the seeds, she lawfully belonged in the Underworld.

Even Zeus could not defy the Fates. However, he worked out a compromise. Persephone would live with Hades in the Underworld for four months of the year and spend the remaining eight months with her mother. (Some myths divide the number of months evenly: six and six.) Thus, the myth explains why the seasons change: When Persephone is with her mother, flowers bloom and crops grow and bear fruit, but when she is with her husband in the Underworld, plants wither and die.

Accessory to the Crime

Even though Zeus did not allow the marriage to take place, some myths say that he was partly responsible for Persephone's abduction. According to these myths, Hades did not kidnap Persephone immediately but pined for her before Zeus helped him devise a plan to steal the girl.

Persephone became the wife of Hades and the Queen of the Underworld. Eventually, she accepted her duties as wife and queen. Some myths even claim that eventually she reciprocated Hades's love.

A MAP OF THE UNDERWORLD

Take a Visit to the House of Hades

G

In Greek mythology, the Underworld was divided into different regions. One region was for the most exceptional mortals (such as heroes), another region was for the common folk, and a third was for evildoers. But there is more to the Underworld than these three main regions, as you will soon see.

INFERNAL GEOGRAPHY

Some early myths situate the Underworld at the very edge of the land of the living, just past the ocean's shoreline. Later, more common myths situate the Underworld beneath the ground. The Land of the Dead was thought to have many entrances, mostly through caves or lakes.

Several rivers surrounded the Land of the Dead, including:

- **Acheron:** River of Woe
- **Cocytus:** River of Wailing
- **Lethe:** River of Forgetfulness
- **Pyriphlegethon:** River of Fire
- **Styx:** River of Hate

You may hear the Underworld itself referred to as "Hades." To the ancient Greeks, Hades was the name of the god, not the place he ruled. The Underworld had several names: the Land of the Dead, the

Nether Regions, the House of Hades, and the Infernal Regions, to name a few. But it was considered bad luck to mention Hades's name or talk about his realm.

ENCOUNTERING CHARON

When a person died, Hermes came to collect that person's shade (or soul) and lead him or her to the Underworld. To get to the Underworld required crossing one or more rivers. To cross a river, the shade had to engage the services of Charon, the ferryman of the dead. Charon didn't work for free; he required a coin as payment. If a would-be passenger could not pay Charon's fee, that shade was doomed to wander the shoreline for a hundred years before being allowed passage. Even after they'd paid and boarded the boat, the shades had to do most of the work—they rowed, while the ferryman merely steered.

Paying the Toll

The ancients had a custom of placing a coin under the tongue of a deceased loved one. This was intended as payment to the ferryman Charon. If someone who died was not properly buried, or not buried at all, that person's shade would wander the river's shore for a hundred years.

After crossing one or more rivers, the shade had to pass Cerberus, the watchdog of Hades, before passing through the Underworld's gates. Cerberus wasn't just any dog. Some myths say he had three heads, while others say he had fifty. Regardless, Cerberus loved to eat raw flesh. Cerberus got along fine with shades on their way into the Underworld; his job was to prevent living mortals from entering and shades from escaping.

THE MAIN REGIONS OF THE UNDERWORLD

After passing Cerberus, the shade came to a fork in the road. From this point, three paths led to different regions of the Underworld. At this fork the shade encountered the Judges of the Dead. Usually the Judges determined which path a shade would take, determining that shade's new home for eternity. Sometimes the gods intervened and made the choice instead. (Hades himself never did this, however.)

Elysium: The Great Resting Place

Elysium (sometimes called the Elysian Fields) was the dwelling place of the exceptional. This island was where heroes (and other extraordinary mortals) were sent after death. Elysium was a paradise, where men and women enjoyed a comfortable afterlife. Games were held, music was played, and good times were had by all. The fields were always green and the sun always shone.

Asphodel Fields: Home for Commoners

Most shades resided in the Asphodel Fields. This region of the Underworld was a middle ground, neither good nor bad. The final dwelling place for most commoners, the Asphodel Fields held more souls than Elysium and Tartarus combined.

Here, the shades normally mimicked the activities of their former lives. Memories did not exist here, so shades usually acted like machines with no individuality. The Asphodel Fields were monotonous and offered little variety or socialization. Even so, this region of the Underworld was a much better place to be than Tartarus.

The Best of Nether Regions

Some myths do not make much of a distinction between Elysium and the Asphodel Fields. Because all shades were merely shadows of a person's former self, none could really grasp what was going on around them. Even so, the ancients believed that Elysium was the best region of the Underworld.

Tartarus: True Hell

Tartarus was located beneath the Underworld. It was so far below ground, in fact, that the distance between Tartarus and the surface was said to be the same as the distance between Earth and the heavens. A dark and dismal place, Tartarus was feared by all, even the gods and goddesses. It was here that the very wicked were sent to suffer eternal punishment.

The Erinyes had the duty of administering severe punishments to the shades assigned to Tartarus. Each Erinye used whips and snakes to torment the evildoers. Sometimes food and drink would be placed before the starving, suffering shadows, and the Erinyes would make sure that the food stayed slightly out of reach.

UNRAVELING THE SECRETS
OF THE UNDERWORLD

Unless you were favored by the gods and sent to Elysium, the afterlife did not hold much promise for mortals. Ordinary people didn't have much to look forward to in death—and evildoers had much to fear.

Religious rites and cults were created to address the bleakness of the afterlife. For example, several cults concentrated on individual deities (such as Demeter or Dionysus). Worshipers hoped that these deities would share the secrets of the Underworld—including a map of the Underworld that warned of its dangerous places—so that they could gain entry to Elysium. For example, the Eleusinian Mysteries, secret rites celebrated every year in honor of Demeter and Persephone, promised participants union with the gods and rewards after death.

Charon, from *The Last Judgment*, by Michelangelo, Sistine Chapel

MYTHS IN ART AND MUSIC

Inspiring Artists and Musicians Throughout the Ages

G R

From its very beginnings to today, mythology has inspired visual artists. Almost any museum you visit will have at least one piece of art—perhaps a painting, a sculpture, or an engraving—related to classical mythology. At its root, mythology formed a basis for ancient religion, and art was an important way to express piety. Statues were erected to honor the gods and goddesses, carvings adorned temple walls, and images were painted on household items such as cups, vases, and plates.

Several Greek and Roman buildings that survive from ancient times are adorned with carvings that depict mythological scenes and characters. Examples include the Parthenon and the Erechtheum in Athens and the temples of the Roman Forum. With a little imagination, you can visualize the scene as it appeared at the height of its popularity.

Numerous classical statues and sculptures still exist today, although many of these have sustained some damage. One of the best-known sculptures is the *Venus de Milo*, currently on display at the Louvre in Paris, which was created between 130 and 100 B.C. Other famous sculptures of gods and goddesses from the classical era that you can see at the Louvre include *Apollo Belvedere* (fourth century B.C.) and the *Winged Victory of Samothrace* (third century B.C.).

During late antiquity and the Middle Ages, the emergence of Christianity replaced mythological subjects in art with images of Jesus, the Virgin Mary, and the saints. With the Renaissance, interest in mythological subjects re-emerged, and artists brought the gods and goddesses back to life in their works. From this period on, many famous works of art depict mythological characters and scenes. Perhaps you're familiar with some of these paintings and sculptures:

- *School of Pan* by Luca Signorelli (1441–1523)
- *The Birth of Venus*; *Venus and Mars* by Sandro Botticelli (1445–1510)
- *Judgment of Paris*; *Venus and Cupid* by Lucas Cranach the Elder (1472–1553)
- *Bacchus and Ariadne*; *The Rape of Europa*; *Danaë*; *The Death of Actaeon* by Titian (c. 1488–1576)
- *Bacchus*; *Medusa*; *Jupiter, Neptune, and Pluto*; *Narcissus* by Caravaggio (1571–1610)
- *Venus and Adonis*; *Prometheus Bound*; *The Rape of Proserpine*; *Venus at the Mirror* by Peter Paul Rubens (1577–1640)
- *Apollo and Daphne*; *The Rape of Proserpina*; *Medusa*; *Aeneas, Anchises, and Ascanius* by Gian Lorenzo Bernini (1598–1680)
- *Penelope at Her Loom*; *Penelope Awakened by Eurycleia* by Angelica Kauffman (1741–1807)
- *Perseus with the Head of Medusa*; *Cupid and Psyche* by Antonio Canova (1757–1822)
- *La Minotaurmachie* by Pablo Picasso (1881–1973)
- *Perseus* by Salvador Dalí (1904–1989)

MYTHS IN MUSIC

Just like artists and writers, musicians and composers have been inspired by classical mythology. Pop songs by artists as diverse as

Rush, U2, the Police, the Indigo Girls, Anthrax, and Suzanne Vega make classical allusions. Bands such as Muse, Throwing Muses, and Venus take their names from classical deities.

In classical music, opera retells the stories of many myths. For example, the story of Orpheus, that consummate musician, has been set to music by Claudio Monteverdi (*L'Orfeo*, 1607), Christoph Willibald Gluck (*Orfeo ed Euridice*, 1762), and Jacques Offenbach (*Orphée aux enfers* [*Orpheus in the Underworld*], 1858).

The story of Troy has also been popular with composers. Hector Berlioz's *Les Troyans* (1858) is a sprawling, five-act grand opera based on the *Aeneid*. Henry Purcell's *Dido and Aeneas* (c. 1689) sets to music the ill-fated love affair of the father of Rome and the queen of Carthage. Other operas that depict events following the Trojan War include Gluck's *Iphigénie en Tauride* (1779), Mozart's *Idomeneo* (1781), and Richard Strauss's *Elektra* (1909).

Strauss's Many Operas

German composer Richard Strauss (1864–1949) mined classical sources for several operas. Besides *Elektra*, he composed *Ariadne auf Naxos* (1912), *Die ägyptische Helena* (1927), *Daphne* (1938), and *Die Liebe der Danae* (*The Love of Danae*, 1940).

ZEUS'S MANY AFFAIRS

Gaining a Reputation with the Ladies

G

Zeus had numerous love affairs before he married Hera, but marriage did nothing to end his philandering. Here you'll read about some of Zeus's many adulterous affairs. Hera had a reputation as the most jealous and vengeful Olympian deity. Read on, and you'll see why.

CALLISTO

The myths vary about the identity of Callisto. Some say she was the daughter of the king of Arcadia; others say she was the daughter of the king of Thebes. Still others say she was a wood nymph. All of the myths agree, however, that she was an attendant of Artemis. Callisto took a vow of chastity, as all attendants of Artemis were required to do. However, Zeus fell in love with her—and you know how that goes.

Because Callisto had vowed to remain a virgin, avoiding the company of all men, Zeus had to disguise himself as Artemis to get close to her. The plan worked, and Zeus had his way with her. Callisto was pregnant with her son Arcas when Artemis discovered that her attendant had broken her vow. For this transgression, Artemis transformed Callisto into a bear and (according to some versions of the myth) later killed her.

AEGINA

Aegina was the daughter of the river-god Asopus. Zeus took a liking to this young girl and transformed himself into an eagle to steal her away. Asopus, furious, searched all over Greece for his daughter. Zeus, however, put an end to this hunt by striking at Asopus with bolts of lightning. Zeus took Aegina to an isolated island, where she conceived a son, Aeacus. After Aeacus was born, Aegina left the island, but asked Zeus to populate it. He granted her wish, and the island bore her name.

A Chip Off the Old Block

Aeacus followed in his father's footsteps. Although he was not a god, he ruled over the island of Aegina. A just and fair ruler, he took justice so seriously that he banished his own sons from the island when they murdered their brother.

ALCMENE

Alcmene was a mortal woman—and married. But she refused to consummate the marriage until her husband, Amphitryon, completed an act of revenge for her. Zeus disguised himself as her husband, saying he'd returned successfully from his mission of revenge. Alcmene welcomed Zeus into her bed, believing he was her husband. One myth states that Zeus ordered the sun god to take a few days off so that their night of lovemaking would last longer.

The real Amphitryon wasn't happy to return to a wife who claimed she'd already slept with him. But because her lover had been Zeus, there wasn't anything a mortal man could do about it. Alcmene's union with Zeus led to the birth of the famed hero Heracles.

DANAE

Danae was the daughter of the king of Argos. According to a prophecy, Danae's son would rise up and kill his grandfather. Knowing this, the king decided to keep Danae away from all men, imprisoning her in a tower with bronze doors. Of course, Zeus wasn't a man; he was a god. Zeus transformed himself into a shower of golden rain and visited Danae. As always, Zeus got what he wanted, and the result was Perseus. He became a great hero.

GANYMEDE

No one was safe from the lust of Zeus, not even young men. Ganymede was a prince of the royal Trojan family. Some myths say that he was the most beautiful of all mortals, men and women alike. When Zeus saw Ganymede, it was love at first sight. Zeus sent an eagle (or transformed himself into an eagle) to carry the youth to Mount Olympus. There, Ganymede became a cupbearer for the gods (particularly Zeus), replacing Hebe in this role.

IO

Io, daughter of the river-god Inachus, was a virgin priestess of Hera. That role should have made her off-limits to Zeus, but he lusted after her anyway. Zeus knew he had to avoid Hera's anger, so he lured Io into the woods. He then covered the area with a large, thick cloud, which concealed their lovemaking. Afterward, he turned Io into a white heifer to hide her. But Hera saw through his ruse.

ELECTRA

Several myths surround Electra, the daughter of Atlas. But none of these myths gives the details of how Zeus seduced her. Even though there isn't a juicy story to narrate their love affair, their union was an important one. Dardanus, son of Zeus and Electra, founded the royal house of Troy.

EUROPA

One day, Zeus looked down from the heavens and saw Europa, daughter of the king of Phoenicia, playing on the beach. He was immediately transfixed by her beauty. Zeus transformed into a glamorous white bull and presented himself to the maiden.

At first, Europa was afraid of the creature, but the bull gently lay down at her feet. Relaxing, Europa petted the creature and then climbed onto his back. Zeus ran off with her, carrying her to the ocean and swimming to the island of Crete. There, he changed back to his true form and made love to Europa beneath a tree. From that time on, the tree was always evergreen. Europa became the first queen of Crete and bore Zeus three sons: Minos, Sarpedon, and Rhadamanthys.

SEMELE

Semele was a mortal woman with whom Zeus fell in love. He came to her disguised as a mortal man, but confided that he was indeed the ruler of the gods. Unlike some of Zeus's other lovers, Semele did not try to escape his advances. They enjoyed a brief love affair, which caused Semele to conceive a son, Dionysus. Zeus promised to give Semele anything she wanted. Taking advantage of this, Semele asked Zeus to show her his true form. But a god's splendor was too much for a mere mortal to bear. When he appeared to Semele in his true form, she burst into flames.

LEDA

Leda was the daughter of the king of Aetolia and the wife of Tyndareus, king of Sparta. Once again, Zeus transformed himself in order to get close to his target—this time, he changed into a swan. Pretending to be fleeing from an eagle, the swan threw itself into Leda's arms. Zeus seduced Leda, and she became pregnant. Leda didn't give birth in the normal way, however. She laid two eggs, from which hatched Polydeuces and Helen (later known as Helen of Troy). Leda had several children—some with Zeus, and some with her husband. Her children included Helen, Polydeuces, Castor, Clytemnestra, Phoebe, Timandra, and Philonoe.

MAIA

Maia was the oldest and most beautiful daughter of Atlas. It was inevitable that Zeus would notice her. To avoid Hera, Zeus snuck away from his sleeping wife at night to visit Maia. She bore him Hermes, who became one of the great Olympians. Maia was lucky; if Hera took revenge on her, the myths don't record it.

TAYGETE

The nymph Taygete was yet another of Atlas's daughters and a companion of Artemis. When Zeus pursued Taygete, she asked Artemis for help, and Artemis turned her into a doe. Zeus had his way with her anyway, making love to Taygete when she was unconscious. As a result, Taygete gave birth to Lacedaemon.

The Pleiades

Atlas had seven daughters by the Oceanid Pleione: Taygete, Electra, Alcyone, Celaeno, Merope, Maia, and Asterope. These divine daughters are known collectively as the Pleiades.

MORE TO LOVE . . .

As the preceding sections suggest, Zeus had many, many trysts during his marriage to Hera—and that's just scratching the surface. As the ruler of the gods and humanity, Zeus was hard to refuse.

But don't imagine that Hera simply stood by and watched her husband's exploits. Even though she was a goddess, she felt the same emotions mortals do—and she felt jealousy particularly strongly. When she was jealous, Hera demanded revenge and punished Zeus's lovers.

ESCAPING DEATH: MORTALS WHO TRAVELED TO THE UNDERWORLD

The Bravest of Souls in the Darkest of Places

G

According to Greek mythology, all shades (souls) traveled to the Underworld, Hades's realm, after death. Although most shades were assigned to the Underworld for eternity, a lucky few did manage to escape. Most were living mortals who went down into the Underworld of their own free will—and with a purpose.

ORPHEUS

Orpheus lost his beloved wife, Eurydice, to a fatal snake bite. He tried to live without her, but his grief was so great that he ventured into the Underworld to retrieve her. Orpheus was a gifted musician, and his music allowed him to reach Persephone, the queen of the Underworld. He used his lyre to charm all the monsters, and even Hades himself.

Persephone took pity on Orpheus and allowed him to take Eurydice back to the land of the living. There was one catch, however—Orpheus could not look back as they made their way out of the Underworld. The pair passed through the Underworld unharmed, but just before they reached their destination, Orpheus was overwhelmed by a desire to look behind him to make sure his wife still followed him. When he looked back, Eurydice was pulled back into the Nether Regions. Orpheus had to return to the land of the living alone.

AENEAS

The Trojan hero Aeneas was visited by his father's ghost, who told his son they would soon meet in the Underworld. So Aeneas set out to visit his father's shade there. Knowing he would not succeed in this mission alone, he sought out the prophetess Sibyl, who agreed to help him.

Before he began his journey, Sibyl advised Aeneas to obtain the talismanic Golden Bough from a nearby wood that was sacred to Persephone. Aeneas did as he was told, and Sibyl led him to the river Styx. Here, Charon was at first reluctant to ferry a living mortal across the river, but Sibyl pointed out the Golden Bough; after seeing it, Charon agreed to give Aeneas passage. Sibyl also helped Aeneas by drugging Cerberus so that Aeneas could pass by. Aeneas passed through several regions of the Underworld and spoke to Dido, the queen of Carthage and his former lover who'd committed suicide when he abandoned her.

Aeneas was able to enter Elysium when he placed the Golden Bough on its threshold as an offering. In the Elysian Fields, he found his father, who showed him the line of their descendants who would found Rome. After visiting with his father, Aeneas was returned to the land of the living.

Odysseus Visits the Underworld

Aeneas wasn't the only hero to venture to the Underworld after the Trojan War. After wandering for many years, the Greek hero Odysseus went into Hades's realm to ask the shade of the prophet Tiresias for advice on getting home. While in the Underworld, Odysseus also spoke with the shades of his mother and of other Greek heroes, including Achilles and Agamemnon.

THESEUS

Theseus's descent into the Underworld wasn't his idea. Unlike the others who journeyed there, Theseus had no great personal mission; rather, he went along to help his friend Pirithous kidnap Persephone. Earlier, Theseus had decided he wanted to marry the famous beauty Helen (who would later become Helen of Troy), so Pirithous had helped him kidnap her. When Pirithous wanted to marry Persephone, Theseus was obliged to return the favor.

The two kings struggled and fought their way through the obstacles of the Underworld and finally reached Hades's palace. Upon arrival, they told Hades that they were going to take Persephone away from him. Hades, greatly amused (and not about to let them succeed), invited them to take a seat. When they did, the men found themselves unable to move. Hades had trapped them in the Chairs of Forgetfulness, where they remained stuck for years. In these chairs, they forgot everything—who they were, where they were, why they were there—and sat motionless, their minds blank.

Later, when Heracles visited the Underworld, he was able to rescue Theseus. Before he could free Pirithous, though, the ground shook violently; Hades was not going to allow the escape of the mortal who'd tried to kidnap his wife. Pirithous remained in the Underworld forever.

SISYPHUS

Sisyphus, king of Corinth, was the cleverest of mortal men—a man who literally outwitted death. During his life, Sisyphus offended the gods, especially Zeus, in many ways. He was greedy, he was a liar, and he often killed guests instead of offering them hospitality. In anger and retaliation, Zeus ordered Hades to imprison Sisyphus in Tartarus, and Hades sent Death (Thanatos) after the mortal.

But Sisyphus fooled Death, chaining up Death with the chains that were intended for Sisyphus. While Death was held prisoner, no mortal could die. Eventually, Ares intervened, because war, his favorite pastime, wasn't much fun for him if no one could die. So Ares freed Death, who turned the tables on Sisyphus.

Before Sisyphus died, though, he made his wife promise that she would deny him proper burial rites, throwing his body into a public square instead of giving him a funeral. She did as he requested, and in the Underworld Sisyphus could not pay the fee to cross the river Styx. He pleaded with Persephone to let him return to the land of the living for three days so that he could punish his wife for her "neglect." The queen of the Underworld granted his request.

Not surprisingly, Sisyphus broke his promise to Persephone and did not return to the Underworld. (He didn't punish his wife, either.) He lived to a ripe old age in complete defiance of the gods. However, since he was a mortal, he eventually returned to the Underworld (some myths say that Hermes dragged him back by force), where he was immediately sent to Tartarus to suffer eternal punishment.

HESTIA

Honorable Hestia, Protector of Families

G R

Hestia, the eldest of the original Olympian deities, was considered the most compassionate, virtuous, and generous. Her worshipers regarded her as pure goodness.

As the goddess of the hearth, Hestia was a family goddess, and every household worshiped her. Hestia protected the home and all family members, and she kept an eye on everything that happened around the house.

Home Is Where the Hearth Is

The hearth was the source of warmth and nourishment because it provided heat for cooking. As a result, to the ancients, the hearth represented the epicenter of the family and one of the most important places in the home.

Although Hestia's primary focus was the home, she was also the protector of communities. In effect, her powers expanded outward from the home to include city halls, civic gatherings, and communal properties. In this sense, she was the goddess of places where people gathered.

Because she was worshiped in the home, Hestia had few temples built specifically in her honor (aside from those of the Vestal Virgins). In her role as protector of a community, public hearths were sacred to her.

Hestia's role as goddess of the hearth also extended to the home of the gods and goddesses. In her devotion to her own home, Hestia spent all of her time on Mount Olympus; unlike her siblings, she did not leave it to traipse about Earth. Even Hades left his home more often than Hestia did.

This reluctance to leave her home may be the reason Hestia doesn't have a myth of her own. Myths rarely mention her, although this silence may be due to the fact that she was a chaste goddess and it was sacrilegious to gossip about her. Or it could be that the exploits of the other gods—filled with love affairs, jealousy, rivalries, and revenge—simply made more entertaining stories.

UNATTAINABLE HESTIA

Like her niece Athena, Hestia loved peace. While Athena would participate in war if necessary, Hestia refused to get involved in any dispute, no matter the cause or the consequences. This strong belief in peace was one reason that Hestia, though essentially goddess of the home and family, did not marry and have a family of her own. Even so, she did have suitors.

Her brother Poseidon and her nephew Apollo, the god of music, both courted her—or at least they wanted to. Rivalry sparked between the two gods, creating a heated argument that had the potential to turn into a larger battle. Hestia, not wanting to be a catalyst for war, refused them both and appealed to Zeus to intervene.

Zeus granted Hestia permission to remain a virgin and offered her his protection. With Zeus on her side, Hestia swore an oath to remain eternally chaste. Her vow of chastity was the reason that she required the Vestal Virgins to be chaste while they served her.

But not everyone respected Hestia's vow of chastity. During a Dionysiac festival, Priapus, son of Aphrodite and Dionysus, saw Hestia and lusted after her. That same night, as Hestia lay sleeping, Priapus attempted to violate her. He nearly succeeded, but a donkey brayed loudly and awoke the goddess. Seeing Priapus, Hestia screamed, and he ran away. From that time forward, the feast of Hestia included adorning donkeys with flowers.

THE TEMPLE OF VESTA

Although most people worshiped Hestia in their homes, one of the most famous temples of the ancient world was erected in her honor: the Temple of Vesta. Located in Rome (Vesta was Hestia's Latin name), this temple was attended by priestesses known as the Vestal Virgins.

In the Temple of Vesta, six priestesses served the goddess. Chosen from the best families of Rome, the priestesses were required to be good-looking, with no physical deformities. They were also required to have two living parents at the time of their appointment. Priestesses of Vesta began their training between the ages of six and ten. The Vestal Virgins were a very important part of Roman culture, and for a child to be chosen was a great honor for the girl and for her family.

BECOMING A VESTAL VIRGIN

A young girl who was in training to become a priestess of Vesta was required to take a vow of chastity and to promise to serve the temple for thirty years. Her initiation included a ceremony in which she was escorted to the temple and met by other Vestal Virgins. They dressed her in white clothing and cut her hair. The training took ten years. After that, the new priestess went into active service for another ten years. During this time, her responsibilities included maintaining the Vestal Fire and sprinkling it with holy water each day. After her active service ended, the priestess spent another ten years training new initiates.

Maintaining the Vestal Fire

The ancient Romans believed that if the Vestal Fire was extinguished, bad luck would come to Rome. Because tending the fire was such an important task, failure was punished severely—a priestess who let the fire go out was beaten with rods.

After thirty years of service to the temple, the priestess could become a private citizen, able to marry and bear children if she desired. However, most Vestal Virgins chose to continue serving the goddess for the rest of their lives. Service to Vesta was, after all, the only life they had ever known.

The Vestal Virgins were treated differently from the common women of Rome. Because they were not under the power of any man, they had some of the same rights men enjoyed. For example, priestesses of Vesta could participate in court trials and create wills to bequeath their belongings to whomever they chose.

DEADLY CONSEQUENCES FOR BREAKING VOWS

The greatest crime a Vestal Virgin could commit was to break her vow of chastity. Doing so was a betrayal of the goddess, but it was also a betrayal of the city of Rome, because Romans believed that the city's well-being depended on the Vestal Virgins' faithfulness. Any priestess caught breaking her vow of chastity was buried alive.

This burial was part of an elaborate ceremony. The disgraced priestess was wrapped in a burial shroud: thin strips of cloth covered with thick linens. This shroud immobilized her and stifled any cries or pleas. Then, she was placed on a stretcher used to carry the dead and conveyed through town in a procession. A priest intoned prayers at the burial site, and the heavy linens were stripped from the woman.

The woman was lowered into the vault, which had been prepared earlier, and placed on a bed. The vault held a single day's worth of water, food, and light. The vault was shut and the grave was filled in. Those participating in the execution were careful to smooth the earth so that no one could tell it was a gravesite.

Because she was buried without the customary burial rituals, it was thought that a disgraced priestess of Vesta would never reach the Land of the Dead. Her sacrifice was meant to appease the deities and prevent any harm from befalling Rome.

DEMETER

The Friendly Agricultural Deity

G

Demeter was the goddess of fertility, grain, and the harvest. As an earth goddess, she preferred to be near the soil, so she didn't spend much time on Mount Olympus. Unlike Hades, however, who stayed within his realm in the Underworld, Demeter participated in the Olympians' councils or tribunals. Her presence, however, was felt most strongly on Earth. More than any other Olympian deity, Demeter could claim to rule Earth because it was her home.

Generally perceived as a kind and generous goddess, she was popular throughout ancient Greece, perhaps because she was thought to spend more time among the people than the other Olympians did or perhaps because her blessing was so important. Her status as the goddess of the harvest and grain meant that the ancients relied on her to provide them with the food they needed to survive. In addition, Demeter held the powers of destruction and creation, so the people wanted to keep her happy.

FACING DEMETER'S WRATH

Although Demeter's basic nature was kind, she felt emotions just as humans did—and her kindness could change to cruelty when she became angry or upset. For example, when Persephone disappeared, Demeter's grief created hardship for humans as well. Another example of Demeter's cruelty is seen in the story of Erysichthon, a foolish young man who felt her wrath.

Erysichthon was the son of the king of Dotion. He decided to build a great hall in which to hold feasts, but he needed timber. Having no respect for the gods, he entered an oak grove that was sacred to Demeter and planned to cut down enough trees to build his banquet hall. As Erysichthon began chopping, blood flowed from the trees' wounds. A passerby warned him not to proceed, but Erysichthon beheaded the man for his meddling. As he continued his attack on the grove, the tree spirits cried out in despair to Demeter.

Demeter disguised herself as a priestess and approached Erysichthon. She begged him to stop destroying the grove, but he ignored her. Next, Demeter ordered him to leave the place. Laughing at the audacity of a mere priestess, Erysichthon threatened her with his ax. Demeter left, telling him to carry on because he was going to need his dining hall.

Demeter was appalled by Erysichthon's blatant act of sacrilege. She called upon Peina (Hunger) to help her punish him. Peina, glad to be of assistance, immediately went in search of the impious young man.

Don't Anger the Gods

Of all the things that mortals might do to offend the gods, blatant violation of something sacred was one of the worst. The sacrilege usually resulted in the offender's suffering and death. Often, as in the case of Erysichthon, the punishment was specially designed to fit the crime. Because Erysichthon violated Demeter's grove to build himself a place to eat, he was tormented by unending hunger.

When she found him, Peina plagued Erysichthon with constant hunger, no matter how much he ate. Within a few days, he'd spent his entire fortune on food—and still was not sated. Everything was gone but his daughter, who sold herself into slavery to buy her father food. Erysichthon was left with absolutely nothing at all. Still tormented by hunger, he began to eat his own legs. Eventually, he killed himself by devouring his own flesh.

As this myth shows, it was never wise for mortals to challenge the gods. Even Demeter, normally a benevolent goddess, could be cruel when crossed.

A PASSIONATE GODDESS

Demeter never married, but she wasn't a virgin goddess like her sister Hestia. The myths tell that Demeter had several lovers.

Zeus

Demeter's first lover was her lustful brother Zeus. Their union produced a daughter, Persephone, and a son, Iacchus. Persephone became Queen of the Underworld. Iacchus was a minor deity who was involved in the Eleusinian Mysteries.

Iasion

Another of Demeter's love affairs began when she attended a wedding. There she met the bride's brother Iasion and instantly fell in love. She called him away from the festivities, and the two made love in a fallow field. When they returned to the wedding, Zeus saw mud on Demeter's back and figured out what they'd done. As punishment, he struck the mortal Iasion with a thunderbolt. Some myths say this attack killed him on the spot; others say it crippled him for life.

During this tryst in the field, Demeter conceived two sons: Plutus and Philomelus. Plutus, meaning "wealth," became the protector of the harvest's abundance. Some myths say that Zeus blinded Plutus to ensure that he would not distribute wealth unevenly among the people. Philomelus was a farmer, content simply to work the land with no desire for riches. The myths say that Philomelus invented the wagon (or the plow, according to some), which was pulled by his two oxen. After his death, Philomelus was turned into the constellation of the Plowman.

Macris

Demeter was also said to be smitten by a young nymph, Macris, nursemaid of the infant Dionysus. Together, Macris and her father nurtured and raised the young god, hiding him from Hera. But Hera eventually found out about the child, whose father was Zeus, and in a fit of jealousy drove Macris from her homeland. Macris took refuge in a cave on a small island.

Demeter came forward to help the persecuted nymph. She taught the people on the island how to plant and harvest corn. The myths never say directly that Demeter and Macris had a love affair, but they suggest that Demeter was quite taken with the nymph.

SEARCHING THE COUNTRYSIDE FOR PERSEPHONE

The best-known myth involving Demeter is the story she shares with her daughter Persephone. Hades abducted Persephone and carried her off to the Underworld. Persephone's screams reached her mother's ears, and Demeter immediately rushed to help her daughter. When she arrived at the site of Persephone's abduction, however, she couldn't find her daughter anywhere. Embarking on a frantic search,

Demeter wandered the entire Earth for nine days and nine nights, carrying a great torch. As she searched, she did not eat, drink, bathe, or sleep.

On the tenth day, she came across Hecate (a minor goddess), who'd heard about the abduction but did not know who had taken Persephone. Hecate led Demeter to Helios, the sun god. As he crossed the sky each day, Helios saw everything that happened in the world below, and he had witnessed Persephone's kidnapping. Helios told Demeter what had happened and tried to reassure her that Hades would take good care of her daughter.

Demeter could not be consoled; she was beside herself with fury, pain, and grief. She abandoned Mount Olympus and her duties as a goddess. Without Demeter's attention, the world was plagued by drought and famine. Plants withered and died, and no new crops would grow.

THE TRAVELING GODDESS

In her grief, Demeter wandered the countryside. Sometimes she encountered hospitality; other times she met with ridicule. For example, a woman named Misme received Demeter in her home and offered her a drink, as was the custom of hospitality. Thirsty, Demeter consumed her drink quickly, and the son of Misme made fun of her, saying she should drink from a tub, not a cup. Angered by his rudeness, Demeter threw the dregs of her drink on the boy, turning him into a lizard.

In Eleusis, Demeter transformed herself into an old woman and stopped to rest beside a well. A daughter of King Celeus invited her to take refreshment in her father's house. Demeter, pleased with the girl's kindness, agreed and followed her home.

At the king's house, Demeter was met with great hospitality from the king's daughter and the queen. Although Demeter sat in silence and would not taste food or drink for a long time, eventually a servant, Iambe, made her laugh with her jokes.

Demeter became a servant in the house of Celeus along with Iambe. The queen trusted Demeter and asked her to nurse her infant son Demophon. In caring for this baby, Demeter found comfort only a child could give her and decided to give the boy the gift of immortality. To do this, Demeter fed him ambrosia during the day and, at night, placed him in the fire to burn away his mortality. But the queen saw the child in the fire and screamed in horror and alarm. Angry at the interruption, Demeter snatched the child from the flames and threw him on the floor.

Demeter changed back into her true form and explained that she would have made the boy immortal, but now he'd be subject to death like other humans. Then, she ordered the royal house to build her a temple and taught them the proper religious rites to perform in her honor. These rites became known as the Eleusinian Mysteries.

COMPROMISING WITH HADES

When Demeter had neglected her duties for nearly an entire year, Zeus realized that he'd have to intervene or the human race would starve. So Zeus went looking for his sister.

When he found her, however, she would not listen to reason. Instead, she demanded that her daughter be restored to her. Demeter refused to relent, and Zeus knew that his only choice was to appease his sister. He ordered Hades to return Persephone. Hades agreed, but he tried to keep Persephone in the Underworld by tricking her into eating some pomegranate seeds.

The gods reached a compromise: Persephone would spend part of the year with her mother on Earth and part of the year with Hades in the Underworld. Her time in each place corresponded with the seasons. While Persephone was in the Underworld, Earth underwent autumn and winter: Crops withered, it grew cold, and nothing would grow. While Persephone was with her mother, however, Demeter's happiness caused plants to grow and ripen.

ATHENA

You Can't Outsmart the Goddess of Wisdom and War

G

Unlike her bellicose half-brother Ares, Athena preferred peace to war. She preferred settling disputes through reason and intelligence. When war was inevitable, however, Athena was a goddess you'd want on your side. Skilled in strategy and warfare, Athena was both a master tactician and a fierce warrior. She was also a prolific inventor and skilled craftswoman.

Athena was the biological daughter of Zeus and Metis. However, Metis didn't physically give birth to Athena. When the love affair between Zeus and Metis resulted in a pregnancy, Gaia came forward and warned Zeus that if Metis had a daughter, she would then have a son. The son would grow to become even greater in strength than Zeus and take over the kingdom of the heavens. Zeus, all too aware of a son's ability to take away his father's power, decided to prevent this birth.

Zeus's solution to the problem? Swallow the mother.

However, when it came time for Metis to give birth, Zeus was struck motionless by a piercing pain in his head. Crying out in suffering, he ordered Hephaestus to use his ax to split open his head to relieve him of the pressure and pain. Hephaestus did as he was told. As soon as the ax split the skull, the daughter of Zeus emerged fully clad in armor. Instead of a baby's wail, the world was met by an adult's war cry.

BRILLIANCE AND MERCY

Athena inherited her mother's wisdom and her father's sense of justice. These two features combined made for a brilliant and merciful goddess. Those in need of aid, especially heroes and soldiers, would call upon Athena's protection. Under her care, characters such as Heracles and Odysseus were able to complete their missions unharmed.

But her realm of protection did not limit itself to people. She was also considered the protector of several cities, including Athens and Argos, and was credited by some with the law and order of civilization. Being wise and just, Athena sat on many councils and took part in her fair share of tribunals. In fact, it is said that she was the one to create the tradition of trial by jury in Athens.

A GODDESS OF MANY TALENTS

As if wisdom and war weren't enough, Athena was also the patron goddess of several other matters: goddess of the arts, including literature, poetry, music, and philosophy. Her very being inspired poetry, and several wrote of her gray eyes and her stately presence.

A Goddess for Weavers

In contrast to the at-times cold hand of intelligence and reason, Athena showed her warmer side by becoming the patron of spinners and weavers. It is said that she invented weaving and other domestic crafts performed by the women of ancient Greece. Just as men were able to relate to her in terms of war and strategy, she enabled the women to feel that same closeness through their own activities.

But it wasn't just the men who participated in battle who knew and respected Athena. She gained the favor of all men in reciprocating the respect due to them for the hard work they endured. Not afraid of hard work herself, she also became the patron of metalworkers, carpenters, and the majority of skilled workers.

VIRGINITY'S CONSEQUENCES

Though she could relate to almost every person on Earth in one way or another, she was unable to relate to those bearing the weight of motherhood. Nor did she ever know what it was to be caught up in the throes of passionate love. Athena was a virgin goddess, and had no desire to be otherwise. This isn't to say she didn't feel emotion, for the goddess certainly was compassionate. But she simply would not allow a passionate love to interfere with her sound judgment, as it seemed to do with nearly every other deity. She did of course enjoy the company of men, but in a fashion of camaraderie only.

ATHENIAN CULTS

As you can imagine, several shrines and temples were built to honor Athena. Nearly everyone had a reason to worship her. And of course, being a protector of several cities, several elaborate sanctuaries were devoted to her alone, the two most popular being the Parthenon and Erechtheum, both of which were located atop the acropolis in Athens.

The Parthenon

The Parthenon is one of the best-known temples of ancient Greece, partially due to the fact that remains of the temple are still standing today. It has become a hot spot for tourists and a hot topic for those studying architecture.

Athena's Temple: The Parthenon

Parthenon means "chamber of the virgin." The temple was built in Athena's honor, but its art depicts other deities (even though they were not worshiped in the temple). The Parthenon contains sculptures of scenes taken from Greek mythology, such as the war between the gods and the Giants.

The Parthenon was built to house a 35-foot-high statue of Athena, made of ivory and gold. This immense temple, though built to honor the goddess Athena, also served to glorify Athens as a whole. Of course, the religious Athenians still honored and worshiped the deities in the Parthenon, but on the whole, it was more for show. Looking at the Parthenon, no one could question the grandeur and wealth of Athens.

The Parthenon was certainly a sight to see. Expensive and elaborate, the temple was quite a display. Even so, it simply did not serve the practical purposes that many of the other temples did. In fact, the traditional rituals and sacrifices were made to the older cult statue of Athena, which was housed in the Erechtheum.

The Erechtheum

The Erechtheum was smaller than the Parthenon and situated nearby. This temple, though not nearly as grand and luxurious as the Parthenon, served a more practical purpose. It was here that the olivewood statue of Athena was placed, the statue that served as part of the Panathenaea festivals.

During midsummer, those wishing to pay tribute to the goddess Athena would gather together on what was thought to be Athena's birthday. Athletic and musical competitions took place, but the greatest event was the dressing of the wooden statue. Every year, a select group of women made a new woolen gown for the statue. During the festival, a great show was made of taking this gown through the city and draping it over the statue in the Erechtheum. Yet another festival involving this statue took place every four years and was called the Great Panathenaea. During this celebration, the statue would be carried to the sea and washed.

ATHENA THE INVENTOR

With such a versatile mind and an array of abilities, Athena was revered for many things and her duties kept her quite busy. However, she did manage to find time to throw in a few inventions here and there. She was fond of mankind and took pleasure in giving the race gifts every once in a while; her inventions were almost always in favor of the human race.

Athena's natural sense toward practicality was illustrated in her toolmaking: The plow, the yoke, and the bridle were all gifts to make life easier and more efficient for the ancients. On a culinary note, she is also credited with introducing olive oil.

Athena is also thought to have overseen the building of the first ship, the *Argo*. Some argue that this wasn't the first ship, but allow that it was the largest ship to have ever been built. (This was the ship used by Jason and the Argonauts during his quest for the Golden Fleece.)

Yet other credits to Athena's name were the introductions of the war chariot, the flute, the trumpet, and the science of mathematics. The list goes on, and the ancients were quite grateful to Athena for her generous presents.

THE JUDGES OF THE DEAD

The Judges and the Judged: Symbolism in the Underworld

Ⓖ

The Judges of the Dead decided the destinies of those who dwelled in the Underworld. Although the Judges were symbolically important to the Underworld, they didn't have much real power. The gods themselves decided whether a person had been wicked enough to send to Tartarus or brave and good enough to spend eternity in Elysium. That meant that the Judges usually sent shades to the Asphodel Fields without much consideration.

AEACUS

Aeacus, son of Zeus and Aegina, was considered to be the most pious of all Greeks. Aegina left her son on a deserted island, which Zeus populated to give the boy companions. He grew up to become the ruler of the island, which was called Aegina after his mother.

Aeacus fathered three sons: Peleus, Telamon, and Phocus. When Phocus grew into a great athlete who was adored by all, his two older brothers grew jealous and murdered him. Aeacus discovered what had happened and banished his two remaining sons from the island, leaving him without an heir.

Because Aeacus prized justice over family and lived a pious, upright life, Zeus decided to honor him after his death, and made Aeacus a Judge of the Dead. As an added honor, Aeacus was named the keeper of the keys to the Underworld.

MINOS

Minos was another son of Zeus, born of Europa. He was a king of Crete and, much like his father, ruled with justice and equity. It is said that his laws were so well considered and so well written that they stayed in force for a thousand years.

However, Minos wasn't the ultimate good guy. He fought with Poseidon, had numerous adulterous affairs, and banished his own brother out of jealousy. Despite some bad personal behavior, he was still renowned for his leadership and dedication to justice. So Minos, too, became a Judge of the Dead after his own death. Among the Judges, he had power to make the final decision.

RHADAMANTHYS

Yet another son of Zeus, Rhadamanthys was Minos's brother. Some myths say that Rhadamanthys ruled Crete before Minos came to power. As ruler, Rhadamanthys established a code of laws that became so popular it found its way into Sparta. Rhadamanthys lost his position as ruler of Crete when he and Minos got into a dispute over the affections of a young boy. Minos was stronger than his brother and drove Rhadamanthys off the island.

After leaving Crete, Rhadamanthys made his way to the Aegean Islands, where his reputation as a great ruler preceded him. He ruled over these islands until his death.

Rhadamanthys also became one of the Judges of the Dead. Some myths claim that he was responsible for settling disputes among the shades. Other myths say that he ruled Tartarus and participated in punishing the inhabitants.

APOLLO

A Tall, Dark, and Handsome God

Ⓖ

Apollo was smart, goodhearted, and a mighty Olympian—but even better, he was tall, dark, and handsome. The ancients usually depicted Apollo as an ideal of masculine beauty: He was tall and muscular, with the charm of youth and long, slightly curling hair. Even though he was physically attractive, the young god was often unlucky in love and suffered numerous rejections. Never fear, though—he had his share of amorous successes as well.

Apollo was highly skilled in many fields of endeavor. He was the god of archery, fine arts, music, religious purity, prophecy, medicine, and eloquence. Although his sister was associated with all wild animals, Apollo had a few select animals as his companions. Most often he was linked with the wolf, even though he was a shepherd and the protector of shepherds and their flocks. He was also connected with deer and with several species of birds, including crows, vultures, swans, and kites.

Apollo was an admirable deity, one to be respected and appreciated. Yet, like his sister (and all of the gods), he could also be harsh. For example, Apollo did not hesitate to commit murder to defend his mother's honor. He also sent plagues to cities that defied him (as the god of medicine, he could inflict illness as well as cure it). Although he wasn't as quick to take revenge as his sister was, Apollo suffered no insults.

MUSICALLY GIFTED

Several myths highlight Apollo's artistic gifts, particularly in his role as the god of music. The Olympians themselves recognized Apollo's musical virtuosity and loved to lounge around Mount Olympus listening to Apollo play his lyre.

One myth that tells of Apollo's musical genius is the story of Marsyas, a satyr from Phrygia. When Marsyas found a double flute that Athena had thrown away, he began to play it. He thought that the flute produced the loveliest sound he had ever heard—and he was willing to bet that its music was even sweeter than Apollo's. So he challenged Apollo to a musical contest.

Apollo accepted Marsyas's audacious challenge. They set some ground rules, selected the Muses as judges, and agreed that the winner could do as he chose with the loser. Apollo would play his lyre, and Marsyas would play his flute.

Athena and the Double Flute

Athena had invented this flute and played it at a banquet on Mount Olympus. But Aphrodite and Hera made fun of the way her cheeks puffed out as she played. The other gods laughed so hard that Athena was compelled to see for herself. She played her flute, looking at her reflection in a stream, and was disgusted by the way it distorted her face. In anger, she cursed the flute and cast it away.

During the first phase of the competition, both played equally well. The Muses declared a draw, which spurred Apollo to tilt things in his own favor. Apollo challenged Marsyas to play his instrument upside down. It is possible to play a lyre this way, but not a flute. Marsyas lost the round.

Some variations on the music contest exist. In one, Marsyas actually won the first round, and Apollo, desperate to avoid defeat, did his upside-down trick. In another, Apollo won by singing as he played, another feat Marsyas could not accomplish while playing the flute.

Apollo chose a severe punishment. He hung Marsyas from a pine tree and skinned him alive. Some myths say that the satyr's blood and tears (or possibly the tears of his friends) formed the river Marsyas. Other myths say that Apollo later regretted the harsh way he'd treated his defeated opponent, so he broke his own lyre and turned the satyr into a river.

APOLLO THE PLAYBOY

Apollo never married, but like most of the other Olympians he had numerous affairs, producing several children. Here are some of Apollo's most famous amorous successes:

- Apollo had a love affair with Coronis, whom Artemis killed for marrying a mortal man. Coronis's son by Apollo was Asclepius, who became a god of healing and medicine.
- Chione was visited by both Hermes and Apollo in the same night. She had a son from each union. With Apollo, she had Philammon, who became a great musician.
- Cyrene was watching her father's flocks when a lion attacked. She wrestled the lion; Apollo saw this act of courage and fell in love. Together they produced two sons: Aristaeus and Idmon.

Aristaeus was the inventor of bookkeeping, and Idmon became a famous prophet.

- Apollo had a tryst with Hecuba, the wife of King Priam. Their love affair produced a son, Troilus. A prophecy predicted that Troy would never fall if Troilus lived to the age of twenty, but he was killed by Achilles during the Trojan War.

- Manto, daughter of the seer Tiresias, was given to Apollo as a war prize. She perfected her prophetic abilities at Delphi and gave Apollo a son, Mopsus, who grew up to become a famous prophet as well.

- Apollo's lover Phthia bore him three sons: Dorus, Laodocus, and Polypoetes. All three were killed by Aetolus to gain control of the country they ruled, which then became known as Aetolia.

- When Rhoeo's father discovered she was pregnant, he assumed that her lover was mortal and punished her by putting her in a chest and setting her adrift in the ocean. But the child was Apollo's, and she landed safely on Delos, Apollo's own birthplace and an island sacred to him. There, she gave birth to Anius, a prophet who became one of Apollo's priests.

- Apollo was closely associated with the arts, so it's no surprise that one of his lovers was a Muse—Thalia, who ruled comedy and idyllic poetry. Their children were the Corybantes, male followers of the nature goddess Cybele.

- Another Muse, Urania, also had an affair with Apollo. Urania was the Muse of astrology and astronomy, and her union with Apollo produced two sons: Linus and Orpheus. Both grew up to be famous musicians.

Although this is only a partial list, you can see that Apollo favored Muses, nymphs, and mortal women as lovers. Surely, his brains, good looks, and many talents helped him unite with so many diverse lovers.

FESTIVALS AT DELPHI: PYTHIAN GAMES

Apollo was famously associated with Delphi, one of the best-known and most influential shrines of ancient Greece. According to one myth, Hera had sent a snake named Python to chase Leto while she was pregnant with Artemis and Apollo. The young Apollo pursued Python to Delphi and killed her. But Gaia, the mother of Python, demanded retribution. To appease Gaia, Apollo founded musical and theatrical festivals at Delphi, naming them the Pythian Games in honor of Python. (He also went to the Vale of Tempe to undergo ritual purification and be cleansed of Python's murder.)

In Delphi, Apollo learned the art of prophecy from Themis, a Titaness who controlled the oracle. (Some myths disagree and say that Pan taught prophecy to Apollo.) Apollo then took charge of the oracle, granting the power of prophecy to a priestess known as the Pythia. At Delphi then, people could receive communication from the gods and learn about their fates.

Apollo's prophecies were delivered by the Pythia, who would go into a trance and allow Apollo to speak through her and answer the supplicants' questions. The oracle was so busy that often the services of three Pythia at a time were required.

A Tricky Oracle

Prophecies given by the Pythia weren't always straightforward. For example, King Croesus of Lydia asked the Pythia if he should invade Persian territory. She replied that if he did invade, a great empire would be destroyed. Croesus assumed she meant that he'd destroy the Persian Empire. Only after he invaded and was defeated did he realize that the "great empire" was his own.

Pilgrims traveled from all over to consult the oracle. However, the divination only took place on nine days during the year: the seventh day of each month, except for three months when Apollo was not present in the sanctuary. Because the demand far exceeded the oracle's ability to answer every question, the pilgrims had to draw lots. Those who were chosen would undergo a purification ritual and then ask their questions. The Pythia would mutter something unintelligible, and a male priest would interpret her words for the supplicant.

The oracle at Delphi remained popular for many years. It began to lose its importance in the first century A.D., as Christianity emerged. In the late fourth century, Emperor Theodosius I banned the old pagan religions, and the oracle was no more.

DIONYSUS

Party Gods Have All the Fun

G

Dionysus was the god of wine and revelry. The ultimate party god, he was always ready for a good time—and he wanted to make sure that his followers shared in the fun. Not surprisingly, Dionysus was a popular god, in worship and in the myths.

THE TWICE-BORN GOD

Different myths tell different stories of Dionysus's birth. Both versions name Zeus as his father and emphasize Hera's jealousy, but the child's mother and the circumstances of his birth differ.

Myth One

During one of his many affairs, Zeus seduced Semele disguised as a human male, although he told her that he was actually the ruler of the gods. Hera learned of their affair and was consumed with jealousy. She disguised herself as an old woman and sought out the pregnant Semele, eventually gaining the woman's trust. When Semele confided that Zeus was the father of her child, Hera made her doubt whether her lover had told the truth.

To discover her lover's actual identity, Semele asked him to grant her a wish. Still smitten with the young woman, Zeus promised her anything she wanted, and Semele requested that he reveal his true form to her. Zeus knew that any mortal who looked upon him as he really was would die and begged her to change her mind. She persisted, and he had no choice but to comply. When he presented himself to her in all his glory, Semele burst into flames.

Zeus called on Hermes to rescue his unborn child. Hermes extracted the baby from the mother while Zeus cut a gash in his own thigh. Hermes placed the child inside Zeus's wound and stitched it back up. Three months later, Dionysus was born.

Myth Two

In this version, Zeus was again Dionysus's father, but Persephone was his mother. Zeus, desiring Persephone, turned himself into a snake and mated with her. From this union, Zagreus was born. The infant boy had horns and came into the world wearing a crown of snakes.

Hera hated Zeus's illegitimate son and wanted to destroy him. She stole the child and handed him over to the Titans, telling them to kill him. In some stories, Zagreus runs from the Titans, changing into different animals as he flees. In the end, though, the Titans tore Zagreus to pieces. They cooked and devoured him—everything except the heart.

Athena intervened, stealing the heart and turning it over to Zeus. Zeus gave Semele the heart and ordered her to eat it. She did as she was told and became pregnant with the child whose heart she'd consumed. When the child was born the second time, he was named Dionysus.

DIONYSUS DRIVEN MAD

Although Hera could not prevent Dionysus's birth, she was determined to seek revenge for her husband's infidelity. Zeus knew his wife, however, and took precautions to protect his son. As soon as Dionysus was born, Zeus placed him in the care of Ino (Semele's sister) and her husband, Athamas, the king of Orchomenus.

To hide Dionysus from Hera's watchful eyes, the couple dressed him as a girl. Eventually, however, Hera saw through the disguise and punished the couple. She drove Ino and Athamas mad, causing them to kill their own sons.

Before Hera could attack Dionysus, Zeus again rescued him. He transformed Dionysus into a young goat and ordered Hermes to take him to Mount Nysa and place him in the care of some nymphs who lived there. Well hidden, Dionysus grew up happy and healthy.

Time passed, and Dionysus was transformed into his true form. Hera, who hadn't given up searching for him, discovered the young Dionysus and drove him mad. For several years, the mad Dionysus wandered through the world. His aimless travels eventually led to the land of Phrygia, where he was taken in by the earth goddess Cybele (also known as Rhea). Cybele cured Dionysus of his madness and initiated him into her religious cult. He stayed with Cybele for a while, learning her rites and practices. Before long, Dionysus had created his own religious cult, using Cybele's as its foundation.

THE RITES OF DIONYSUS

The religious rites of Dionysus were different from those held to honor other Olympian deities. Traditional rites honored the gods and goddesses in temples specially built for that purpose. Dionysus wandered among the people, and his cults celebrated him in the woods. In Dionysian festivals, worshipers became one with the god.

Dionysus was usually accompanied on his travels by the Maenads, wild followers whose name means "madwomen." The Maenads carried a thyrsus, a symbol of Dionysus, and incited people to join Dionysus's cult and participate in his rites. Although everyone was invited, women were the most eager participants in Dionysian festivals.

What Was a Thyrsus?

A thyrsus was a long pole or rod covered in grapevines or ivy, adorned with grapes or other berries, and topped with a pinecone. It was a symbol of fertility and a sacred object in Dionysian rites.

Dionysus was the god of wine, and his rituals celebrated this drink. It was believed that wine gave people the ability to feel the greatness and power of the gods. Through wine, his worshipers achieved the ecstasy they needed to merge with the god.

Dionysian rites were usually held at night. Women dressed in fawn skins, drank wine, wore wreaths of ivy, and participated in wild dances around an image of Dionysus (believed to be the god himself). Sometimes the women would suckle baby animals such as wolves or deer, and sometimes they would hunt down an animal, tear it to pieces, and devour the raw meat. Occasionally, the crazed women would tear apart a man or a child in their rites.

The wine and tumultuous dancing took worshipers to a state of ecstasy, in which they felt the power of the gods. Religious ecstasy was often heightened by sexual ecstasy. The nights were wild and the followers frenzied—and anything was possible.

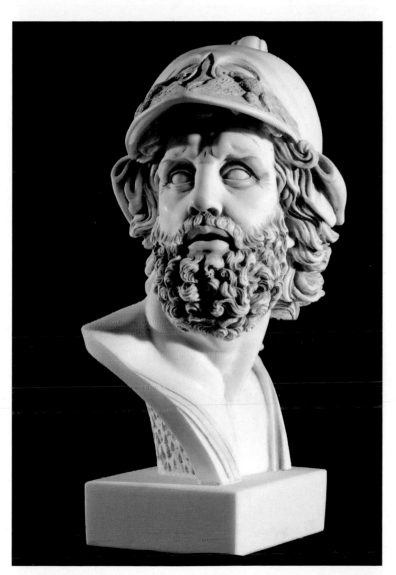

A bust of Zeus, widely considered the most powerful God in ancient Greek religion.

The Birth of Venus by Sandro Botticelli remains the most iconic rendering of Venus, the Roman goddess of love.

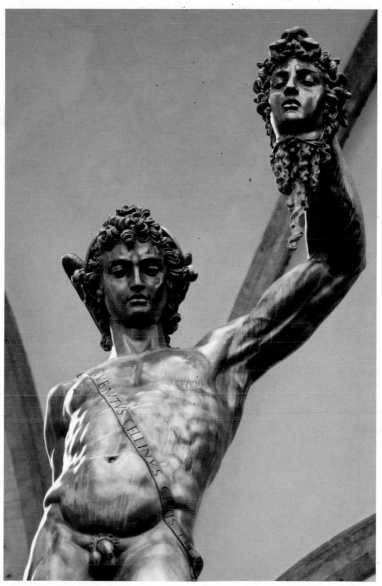

Perseus, "the most renowned of all men," holding the head of Medusa. This rendering by Antonio Canova remains on display at The Vatican.

Located in Athens, construction on the Parthenon began in 447 B.C. and remains an example of classic Greek architecture to this day.

Aphrodite, the Greek goddess of love.

The Return of Persephone by Frederic Leighton displays the "forced love" between Persephone and Hades, the lord of the underworld.

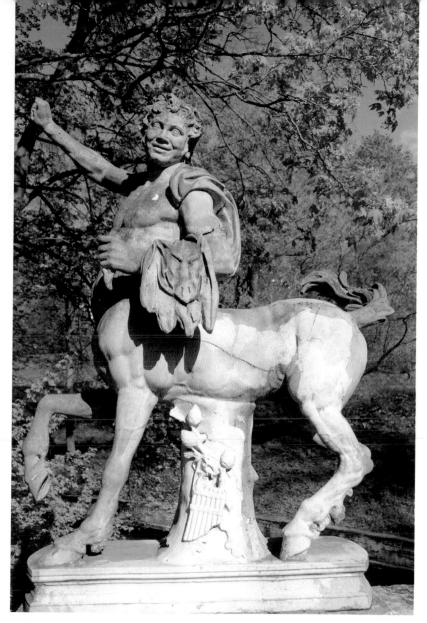

A sculptor's rendering of a Centaur. A frequent subject in Greek art, Centaurs appeared in both the *Iliad* and the *Odyssey*.

Two depictions of Juno, the daughter of Saturn. Known in Greek mythology as "Hera," Juno became known as the goddess of marriage, protecting wives and women in general.

DIONYSUS TAKES A WIFE

Ariadne, daughter of the Cretan king Minos, was in love with the great hero Theseus. When Theseus came to Crete to kill the Minotaur, Ariadne fell in love with him at first sight. Unfortunately, the feeling wasn't mutual.

Ariadne helped Theseus achieve his quest, thus alienating herself from her father. She ran off with Theseus, who promised to marry her when they reached Athens. On their journey, they stopped at the island of Naxos. As Ariadne lay sleeping on the shore, Theseus sailed away and left her.

She awoke alone and friendless on a strange island, abandoned by her lover. But Dionysus saw her and was struck by her beauty. He fell in love with her instantly, as Ariadne had done with Theseus, and he made her his wife. Some myths say the couple resided on the island of Lemnos; others say he took his bride to Mount Olympus.

Ariadne and Dionysus had many children, including Oenopion, Phanus, Staphylus, and Thoas. Oenopion became the king of Chios. Phanus and Staphylus were Argonauts who accompanied Jason on his quest. Thoas became the king of Lemnos.

PUNISHING HIS OFFENDERS

Although the Dionysian rites were popular, not everyone accepted them. Some held that Dionysus wasn't truly a god, a claim that stirred his wrath. Just as Hera had punished Dionysus with madness, he punished those who offended him in the same way. Then, he'd watch as the afflicted mortal destroyed himself.

Beware Dionysus's Wrath

Dionysus, though a good-time guy, had a short temper and a creative imagination. His punishments were cruel and brutal—and not just for the one being punished. Sometimes, innocent bystanders also got hurt.

THE GOLDEN TOUCH

Although Dionysus could be cruel to those who crossed him, he was also a much-loved god who often rewarded his followers. Dionysus's favorite gift to bestow was wine. From time to time, however, he allowed the recipient to choose the gift. The story of King Midas is one example.

Dionysus's companion and tutor, Silenus, was captured by the people of Lydia and taken to King Midas of Phrygia. Midas recognized Silenus as a companion of Dionysus and welcomed him into his household. The king entertained Silenus for ten days and ten nights, going above and beyond the rules of hospitality. Then, he sent Silenus back to Dionysus, accompanied by an escort.

To thank the king for his hospitality to Silenus, Dionysus offered Midas whatever gift he desired. Midas requested that anything he touch turn to gold. Dionysus reluctantly granted the king's wish.

At first, Midas was pleased with his newfound ability. He reveled in his ability to turn ordinary objects like stones and twigs into solid gold. When he sat down to eat, however, Midas realized the problem with his wish. When he tried to eat, his food and drink turned to gold. In despair, Midas realized that his gift was going to kill him.

He called on Dionysus to take back this gift, and the god advised Midas to bathe in the river Pactolus. Midas did as he was told. When he touched the river, his power to turn objects into gold flowed into the water, and the sands of the river became golden. The river became known as a rich source of gold.

JOINING THE OLYMPIANS

Although Dionysus loved to wander the Earth and spend time with mortals, he did take his place on Mount Olympus as one of the twelve great deities. Before he left for the heavens, he undertook a personal quest to retrieve his mother.

In one version of his myth Dionysus's mother Semele died before she could give birth to him. Although Dionysus never knew his mother, he was driven to find her. That was a difficult task because she dwelled in the Underworld.

Still, Dionysus was determined. He consulted a guide, who told him to enter the Underworld through the Alcyonian Lake, a route much faster than traveling by land. When he reached the Underworld, Dionysus had to bargain with Hades to get his mother back. He traded one of his own sacred plants, the myrtle, to Hades in exchange for his mother's freedom. Semele was released from the Underworld and accompanied her son to Mount Olympus, where Dionysus took his place among the great Olympians. Dionysus reconciled with Hera, and Semele was permitted to live in luxury among the gods.

ARES

The Fearsome Warrior Who Needs to Learn Some Manners

ⓖ

Ancient battlefields were places of confusion, bravery, violence, brutality, and bloodlust. They were also where Ares, god of war, felt most at home. Ares loved nothing more than a good fight; he represented the violence and chaos of war. Ares would rather use his weapons than his brain; this god was all about muscle and brute force.

AN ABOMINABLE DEITY

As the son of Zeus and Hera, Ares deserved respect. As this divine child grew older, however, he developed a repugnant personality. Even though he was one of the twelve great Olympians, not many could bring themselves to like Ares—not even his parents.

Ares cared for nothing but battle and bloodshed. He had no interest in ideals of justice or the strategic challenges of war. Instead, he strove to heighten war's terror and destruction. Most myths associate him with the spirit of war itself and show him without morality, principles, or decency.

Ares certainly looked the part of a fearless, brutal warrior. A tall, musclebound god who towered over mortals, Ares always wore armor and a helmet and carried a shield and either a sword or a spear (sometimes both). Ares was known for his terrible war cry, which he would loose before or during a battle, striking fear into the hearts of his enemies.

Despite his fearsomeness, Ares lacked cleverness and wisdom. A god of action, Ares lived for the excitement of battle and bloodshed, but he avoided strategizing. Since he was unwilling to think things through, he was easily outwitted.

THE WILD ONE

Ares lived in Thrace, a land beyond the borders of Greece located north of the Aegean Sea. The Thracians didn't speak Greek, but their language appealed to Ares even more: They spoke the language of war.

The Thracians were divided into tribes, and each tribe had a warlord. The Greeks saw the Thracians as a rowdy race, known for becoming intoxicated and picking fights. The Thracians were skilled, savage warriors who wielded heavy swords and were ferocious in battle. This is why the Greeks regarded Thrace as the ideal dwelling place for Ares—he could live there among bloodthirsty, war-loving bullies.

ARES'S ATTENDANTS

Although Ares was unpopular among gods and mortals alike, he wasn't a complete loner. The myths often describe him in the company of one or more of these attendants:

- **Deimos:** Personification of fear
- **Enyo:** Goddess of battle
- **Eris:** Personification of discord
- **Phobos:** Personification of terror

These four beings often helped Ares prepare for battle. As Ares created a fog of fury that filled warriors on both sides with the desire for battle, his four companions would work to spread terror and discord among them. The work of Ares's attendants made the battle even more bloody and desperate.

LOVERS FOR THE GOD OF WAR

Although Ares was generally hated and feared (as war itself is), he still had several love affairs. In particular, the goddess Aphrodite was one of the few who truly loved him. Ares also had a few other conquests on the field of love.

Opposites Attract: Loving Aphrodite

The best known of Ares's love affairs was with Aphrodite, goddess of love, a case of "opposites attracting." Aphrodite was the only Olympian deity who cared for Ares. Their love affair was passionate and rather scandalous.

Together they had four children, although some myths put the total at five. Deimos and Phobos, sons of Aphrodite and Ares and the personifications of fear and terror, delighted in accompanying their father to battles. Anteros, another son, grew up to become the god of passion and was sometimes also called the god of tenderness. Harmonia, a daughter, was later given in marriage to Cadmus, king of Thebes.

Eros's Lineage

Some myths claim that Eros (god of love) was another son of Ares and Aphrodite. Other myths, however, say that Eros was born during creation.

Aglaurus

Aglaurus was a name shared by a mother and her daughter. Ares fell in love with the daughter. Her father was Cecrops, a king of Athens. The union of Aglaurus and Ares produced a daughter, Alcippe. Later, the son of Poseidon raped Alcippe, an act that eventually led to Ares's trial for murder.

Cyrene

Cyrene, a nymph, was the daughter of the king of Lapithae. Her affair with Ares produced a son named Diomedes, who would become the king of the Bistones in Thrace. He was best known for his four savage mares, which he fed human flesh each day. Diomedes shows up later in a myth of Heracles.

Demonice

By Demonice, Ares had four sons: Evenus, Molus, Pylus, and Thestius. Evenus became the king of Aetolia and had a river named after him. Molus met an untimely death when he tried to rape a nymph and was beheaded. Pylus was not well known, and Thestius became a king in Aetolia.

Aerope

Ares fell in love with a young mortal woman named Aerope. The myths don't record much about their love affair aside from the fact that they had a son together. Sadly, giving birth to a god's son was too much for this young woman and she died in childbirth. The child survived, however; Ares made sure the baby was able to suckle from his dead mother's breasts.

Harpinna

Harpinna was the daughter of Asopus, a river-god. The union of Ares and Harpinna produced a son, Oenomaus, who grew up to become king of Pisa. He also founded a city, which he named after his mother. (Some myths claim that Sterope, one of the Pleiades, and not Harpinna was the mother of Oenomaus, but in these myths Ares is still his father.)

Otrere

Otrere was queen of the Amazons. She gave birth to Ares's daughter Penthesilea, who later took her mother's place as the Amazons' queen. During the Trojan War, Penthesilea was slain in battle by Achilles. After Achilles had stripped the dead queen of her armor, he fell in love with her beauty and was saddened by her loss.

Who Was Achilles?

Achilles was the son of Peleus, king of Phthia, and Thetis, a sea goddess. Achilles was considered the greatest Greek warrior of the Trojan War, earning this acclaim by slaying Hector, the greatest Trojan warrior.

Protogenia

Protogenia was the daughter of Calydon and Aeolia. Calydon, a great hero, was held in such high regard that a city in Aetolia was named after him. Aeolia herself was a famous heroine. You'd think that Protogenia's bloodline, combined with an Olympian's, would add another hero to the family, but she and Ares produced Oxylus, a rather ordinary child.

Chryse

The union of Ares and Chryse led to a son, Phlegyas. One myth says that Phlegyas's daughter was violated by Apollo. When Phlegyas learned of the rape, he set fire to Apollo's temple at Delphi. Apollo, appalled by this act of sacrilege, shot and killed Phlegyas. Then Apollo sent Phlegyas to the Underworld, where the mortal suffered the eternal torment of being beneath a huge boulder that could fall and crush him at any moment.

Pyrene

The union of Ares and Pyrene produced a son, Cycnus, who inherited his father's bloodlust. Cycnus murdered pilgrims as they traveled to Delphi and used his victims' skulls to build a temple to his father. Cycnus is most famous for battling Heracles. Ares's son didn't stand long against the hero, who was aided by Athena. Angered by the death of his son, Ares tried to take revenge on Heracles, but Zeus intervened, using his thunderbolts. The death of Cycnus was never avenged.

ARTEMIS

Wild Goddess on the Hunt

G

Daughter of Zeus, Artemis took her place among the twelve great Olympians as the goddess of archery and hunting. She was the elder twin sister of Apollo, and brother and sister were devoted to each other. A virgin goddess, Artemis valued her own chastity and demanded chastity of her followers. She was usually depicted as a young, untamed, independent woman, roaming the forests and mountainsides and forever on the hunt.

As the daughter of Zeus and Leto, Artemis was one of many who suffered Hera's jealous fury. During Leto's pregnancy, Hera sent Python, a great snake, to chase Leto. Leto managed to escape, but when it was time to give birth, she had a difficult time finding someone to shelter her because all were afraid of Hera's wrath. Eventually, Leto found refuge with her sister Asteria on the island of Ortygia, where she gave birth to Artemis. As soon as Artemis was born, the girl was strong enough to help her mother cross the sea to the island of Delos and assist her in giving birth to her brother Apollo. Apollo later strangled Python (or shot her with arrows) to punish the snake for pursuing his mother.

The Goddess of Childbirth

Because she helped her mother during the birth of Apollo, Artemis was revered as a goddess of childbirth, watching over mothers who were in labor. Legend had it that women who died in childbirth were actually killed by the arrows of Artemis.

Zeus favored his young daughter and told her to ask for anything she wanted. At the age of three, Artemis asked for three things: a bow and arrows, all the mountains on Earth as her home, and eternal virginity. Zeus granted all she asked. Along with these gifts, he also granted her thirty cities.

Hera, of course, was jealous of the attention Zeus paid to a child he'd had with another woman. So she tormented the young girl by insulting her, spilling her arrows, and striking her. Perhaps it was due to Hera's ill treatment that Artemis grew into a strong-willed woman who was quick to punish those who crossed her.

Aside from Hera's torment, Artemis had a happy existence. She roamed the mountainsides in the company of her nymphs, hunting, and occasionally punishing those who offended her.

A DEVOTED DAUGHTER

Artemis could be harsh and even cruel, but one of her greatest qualities was her complete and unreserved devotion to her mother. Both she and Apollo recognized the difficulty their mother had had in bringing them into the world, and they respected no one more than her. Throughout the myths Artemis and Apollo joined forces to protect their mother or to seek revenge on those who bothered her.

PROTECTING LETO

Filled with jealousy and recognizing that she could not prevent the birth of the divine twins, Hera still wanted to punish Leto. While the twins were away from their mother, Hera filled the Giant Tityus with lust for Leto. Acting on his desires, Tityus tried to rape Leto, but Leto cried out to her children, who rushed to her aid. The two shot their arrows at Tityus and killed him before he could violate their mother.

After his death, Tityus was sent to Tartarus. This Giant was so huge that, when he was secured to the ground, his body covered several acres (between two and nine, depending on the myth). Every day, a pair of vultures tore out his liver and ate it, but it grew back every night.

AN EASILY OFFENDED GODDESS

Artemis was not one to take insults and perceived slights lightly. She could be merciless in punishing those who offended her in any way.

Adonis was a beautiful young man who was loved by Aphrodite. Out of jealousy, Ares took the form of a boar and gored Adonis to death. Other myths name Artemis responsible for Adonis's death. In one, Artemis punished Adonis's boast that he was a better hunter than she was by sending a wild boar to kill him. In another, Aphrodite caused the death of Hippolytus, a hunter who'd scorned her to serve Artemis instead. Artemis then killed Adonis in retaliation for the death of Hippolytus.

Agamemnon, commander of the Greek forces during the Trojan War, was already disliked by Artemis because of his family's history. (His father, Atreus, had promised to sacrifice his best lamb to Artemis but broke that promise when he found and hid a golden lamb, keeping it for himself.)

Before sailing for Troy, Agamemnon went hunting and killed a deer in a grove sacred to Artemis. Impressed with his own accomplishment, Agamemnon boasted that his skill as a hunter was equal to—or even better than—that of Artemis. The goddess, offended by both his act and his boast, decided to punish Agamemnon.

Artemis prevented the winds from blowing, so Agamemnon's fleet could not sail to Troy. She refused to relent unless Agamemnon made a sacrifice to her, but she didn't want just any sacrifice. Artemis demanded that he sacrifice his eldest daughter, Iphigenia.

Agamemnon sent for his daughter. The myths differ on what happened next. Some say that Agamemnon did indeed sacrifice his daughter to Artemis so the winds would blow again. Others say that Artemis took Iphigenia to Tauris (where she became a priestess in Artemis's temple) and left a deer or goat in her place to serve as the sacrifice.

A VIRGIN GODDESS

Artemis was the third of the virgin goddesses, the other two being Hestia and Athena. As you know, Zeus had granted Artemis the right to remain a virgin forever. Keeping her virginity, however, wasn't as simple as taking a vow of chastity. Artemis sometimes had to fight off would-be suitors.

The Giants Otus and Ephialtes were so strong that not even the gods could hurt them. These brothers successfully kidnapped Ares and then decided they should rule the universe. So they built a mountain as tall as Mount Olympus and demanded that the gods surrender to them. They also demanded two goddesses for their wives: Ephialtes claimed Hera, and Otus claimed Artemis. The gods could not defeat these Giants in battle, so Artemis decided to trick them.

When the brothers were out hunting, Artemis transformed herself into a deer and ran between them. Each Giant threw his spear at the deer, but Artemis leaped out of the way. The spears hit the Giants instead, and in this way the brothers killed each other.

The Ancient Rite of Virginity

To the ancient Greeks, virginity meant more than abstinence from sex. When a woman married, she moved into her husband's home and became subject to him. Virgin goddesses such as Artemis and Athena remained free of men's control, enabling them to live independently and to pursue traditionally masculine activities such as hunting and warfare.

Artemis valued her own virginity so highly that she required her attendants to be chaste as well. When a woman associated with Artemis broke her vow, she was punished severely—even if she'd broken that vow unwillingly.

Callisto, one of Artemis's attendants, had vowed to remain chaste throughout her life. One myth states that Callisto was so committed to Artemis that she shunned all contact with men. However, Zeus lusted after her, and when Zeus wanted a woman he usually got his way. But Callisto's avoidance of men made this conquest a challenge.

To approach Callisto, Zeus disguised himself as Artemis. Callisto, of course, allowed Artemis into her presence and was shocked to find herself face to face with Zeus. Zeus raped Callisto and then left her.

Unfortunately, Callisto became pregnant from the rape. One day, when Artemis and her attendants were bathing in a spring, Callisto had to undress and join them. When she saw Callisto naked, Artemis realized that her attendant was pregnant. In her anger, she transformed Callisto into a bear. Artemis then shot and killed the bear (although she may have been persuaded to do so by the ever-jealous Hera). Zeus, knowing Callisto's death was his fault, felt remorse and changed her into the constellation of the Great Bear (Ursa Major).

What Happened to Callisto's Baby?

Zeus did not want his child destroyed, so he sent Hermes to rescue the child from Callisto's womb immediately after her death. The child, Arcas, grew up to become the king of Arcadia. In some versions of Callisto's story, she gives birth to Arcas while she's still alive (and in bear form). Later, Arcas nearly killed his mother, but Zeus prevented him. Arcas eventually became the constellation known as the Little Bear (Ursa Minor).

WILD BUT LOYAL

Artemis was a complex character, a goddess who inspired admiration and fear in mortals. She exhibited loyalty (as to her mother) and harshness (punishing anyone who offended her or wronged those she loved). She was quick to take offense and could be fierce in her revenge. Although Artemis was a hunter, she felt great love and respect for the animals she hunted, protecting them from mistreatment.

As a virgin goddess, Artemis was independent; she knew what she wanted and went after it. She was free-spirited and closely bound to nature. Her depictions in ancient art suited her well: a young woman dressed in a short tunic, carrying a bow and arrows and as wild as the countryside she roamed.

APHRODITE

The Ancient Queen of Hearts

G

Aphrodite, the goddess of love, emphasized passion and desire over the more spiritual forms of love, and her myths offer some of the juiciest reading of the ancient world.

The myths give different versions of Aphrodite's birth. Some myths say she was the daughter of Zeus and Dione, an Oceanid. But the best-known version says that Aphrodite preceded the other twelve Olympians. This makes sense, because physical love is one of the oldest and strongest forces of human experience.

According to one myth, Gaia, mother of Cronus, persuaded her son to overthrow his father, Uranus. One night, Cronus attacked Uranus, cut off his genitals, and tossed them into the sea. When they hit the water, foam gathered. From this foam emerged Aphrodite, beautiful and fully grown. She made her way to land, where her steps created a trail of flowers.

Ditzy Deity or Loving Soul?

In Greek mythology, Aphrodite was often portrayed as a rather dimwitted, ridiculous deity with a great capacity for cruelty. The Romans (who called her Venus) saw her differently: Venus is portrayed as a goodhearted soul who is more interested in the seriousness of love than in wanton sexual desire.

Regardless of her origin, Aphrodite was the undisputed goddess of love. As you may have read, some of the Olympian deities had multiple duties, but Aphrodite's only job was to make love. She approached this duty with gusto. Because the Greeks associated several other qualities with physical love, Aphrodite was also the goddess of beauty, desire, and sex.

A powerful goddess, Aphrodite held sway over mortals and immortals alike. She could make anyone desire anyone else (except for Athena, Hestia, and Artemis, because the virginity of these goddesses was protected). Aphrodite took great pleasure in helping young mortals obtain their beloved. She also enjoyed making the immortals squirm by causing them to fall in love with each other or with a mortal. Of course, Aphrodite herself was also subject to love. This goddess loved many beings, both mortal and immortal, although she had a particular fancy for mortal men.

Zeus's greatest weapon was the thunderbolt. Poseidon's greatest weapon was the trident. Aphrodite's greatest weapon, however, was a girdle. This wasn't the kind of undergarment some women wear to look slimmer; rather, it was a sash or belt—a magical one. Any woman who wore this magic girdle became irresistible to all who saw her. In moments of generosity, Aphrodite lent her girdle to others. For example, she sometimes let Hera borrow the girdle to seduce Zeus or to reconcile quarreling spouses.

Although Aphrodite was the goddess of sensual love and desire, which often occur outside marriage in the myths, she was also a wife. She and her husband, Hephaestus, were opposites in many ways: She was beautiful, graceful, fickle, and spent her time making love; he was ugly, lame, stable, and spent his time working. Even though it's often said that opposites attract, these two didn't get along.

SHARING HER LOVE

Hephaestus genuinely loved and desired his beautiful wife and never wanted to be apart from her. But Aphrodite couldn't help her nature, and she continued to cheat on her husband—not just with Ares, but with others as well.

Butes and the Siren Mishap

Butes's mother was Zeuxippe, daughter of the river-god Eridanus; his father was either Teleon or Poseidon. Butes was one of the Argonauts who accompanied Jason on his quest for the Golden Fleece. He was also a priest of Athena.

Sailing on the *Argo*, the Argonauts encountered the Sirens, bird-women with beautiful voices. The Sirens' alluring songs mesmerized sailors and caused them to run their ships onto the treacherous rocks. When the Argonauts heard the Sirens, the entire crew resisted their call—except Butes, who fell completely under their spell. When the crew wouldn't steer the *Argo* toward their music, Butes jumped overboard and tried to swim to the Sirens.

Butes would have perished, but Aphrodite saw his plight and took pity on him. She rescued Butes from the sea and took him to Sicily, where the two made love. Aphrodite and Butes had a son, Eryx. (Some myths name Poseidon as Eryx's father.)

Gorgeous Adonis

Aphrodite's most famous mortal lover was Adonis, an incredibly handsome man who was born as the result of an incestuous relationship between Myrrha and her father, King Theias of Assyria. (Other myths name other men as her father, including King Cinyras of Cyprus.) When Myrrha's mother bragged that her daughter was more beautiful than Aphrodite, the goddess caused the girl to feel an unquenchable lust for her own father. King Theias repulsed his daughter's advances but was fooled one night when she disguised herself as a concubine and managed to seduce him. When Theias learned that his daughter was pregnant with his child, he chased her with a knife, intending to kill her. As she fled, Myrrha prayed to the gods for help and was changed into a myrrh tree.

Adonis was born from the tree's trunk. When Aphrodite came across the baby, she was taken with the child's beauty. She put him in a box and delivered him to Persephone in the Underworld. Adonis grew into a handsome young man, and Aphrodite wanted him back, but Persephone didn't want to give up the boy she'd raised. Zeus intervened, saying that Adonis would split his time between the two goddesses.

Aphrodite was so obsessed with her beautiful lover that she wanted to spend every moment with him. Ares grew jealous, took the form of a boar, and killed Adonis. (Some myths say that Artemis sent the boar to avenge Hippolytus, one of her favorite huntsmen, whose death Aphrodite had indirectly caused.) The grieving Aphrodite transformed the blood of Adonis into anemone flowers and decreed that an annual festival would be held in his honor. Adonis's shade returned to the Underworld.

Affairs with Other Gods

Aphrodite also had love affairs with gods. Some myths claim that Ares and Aphrodite shared more than mere physical desire. Although no one else cared for Ares, he was Aphrodite's true love. Together, they had four children: Anteros, Deimos, Phobos, and Harmonia. Some myths say that Eros was also the child of this divine couple.

Aphrodite had affairs with other Olympian gods. Hermes manipulated her into a sexual liaison. She also had affairs with Dionysus (which, according to some myths, resulted in the birth of Priapus) and with Poseidon.

Who Was Priapus?

Priapus was a god of fertility, the son of Aphrodite and (depending on which myth you read) either Dionysus, Hermes, Zeus, or Pan. Priapus had an ugly, gnarled body and unnaturally huge genitals.

LOVE'S HELPING HAND

Throughout the ancient Greek myths, Aphrodite uses her divine powers to further the cause of love. When someone (usually a mortal man) was spurned by his beloved, Aphrodite often stepped in to help him—sometimes even when the man didn't want her help.

Paris and Helen

Perhaps the most famous lovers brought together by Aphrodite were Paris, the handsome son of the king of Troy, and Helen, wife of Menelaus and the woman who would become known as Helen of Troy. Why did Aphrodite bring these two together? The answer lies in an event that happened before Paris and Helen ever laid eyes on each other.

At a wedding attended by the Olympians, the goddess Eris (whose name means "strife") threw a golden apple into the midst of the festivities. The apple was desirable in itself, but it was also inscribed with the words "for the fairest." Three goddesses—Aphrodite, Athena, and Hera—claimed the apple. Each believed that she was the fairest, and an argument broke out. Zeus decreed that a judge would settle the dispute. He told Hermes to lead the three goddesses to Paris, who would serve as judge and choose the winner.

Paris couldn't decide who deserved the prize, so each goddess tried to bribe him. Athena offered him wisdom and victory in battle; Hera promised him power and dominion over Asia; and Aphrodite promised him the most beautiful woman in the world. Paris considered each gift and then awarded the golden apple to Aphrodite.

Aphrodite became the young man's protector. She also kept her promise and helped Paris kidnap Helen, who was already married to King Menelaus of Sparta. Paris made his way to Sparta and visited Menelaus's court. There, Aphrodite worked her magic and caused Helen to fall madly in love with the handsome guest. The couple eloped, causing the Trojan War.

Aeneas and Dido

Aeneas was the son of Aphrodite and Anchises. After the Trojan War, Aeneas traveled to the city of Carthage in Africa. Deeply concerned for the safety of her son, Aphrodite caused Dido, queen of Carthage, to fall helplessly in love with him. Dido extended her protection to Aeneas, allowing him and his men time to rest and replenish their supplies. Dido and Aeneas met at a cave to make love.

Dido truly loved Aeneas and wanted to marry him. Aeneas, however, wanted to continue his journey. When the Trojans were ready to leave, Aeneas left with them. Distraught by his departure, Dido threw herself into a fire.

STILL A MYSTERY: THE ELEUSINIAN RITES

A Secret Cult for Demeter and Persephone

G

The Eleusinian Mysteries, religious rites held in honor of Demeter and Persephone, were the most sacred ritual celebrations in ancient Greece. Eleusis was the city where Demeter stayed while she was in mourning for her daughter. The people built a temple in her honor, where the Eleusinian Mysteries were observed.

The cult was a secret cult, and so it was considered a mystery religion, in which only initiates may participate in rituals and are sworn to secrecy about what happens during those rituals. At Eleusis, stipulations existed about who could be initiated. For example, any person who had ever shed blood could not join the cult. Women and slaves, however, were allowed to participate, even though other sects excluded these groups.

The Eleusinian initiates took their pledge of secrecy seriously and were careful to honor it. In fact, they did such a good job of maintaining silence that today's scholars do not know what happened in the Eleusinian rites, although there are many theories. There were two sets of rites: the Lesser Mysteries (which corresponded with the harvest) and the Greater Mysteries (which corresponded with the planting season and took ten days to complete).

HEPHAESTUS

The Ugly God You'll Root For

Ⓖ

Hephaestus was a lucky deity: He was married to Aphrodite, the goddess of love, passion, and desire. You'd think the goddess of carnal love would be married to a sexy, attractive man. Not so. Hephaestus was a master craftsman, but he was ugly and walked with a limp. They were the original odd couple.

SPURNED BY HERA

Hephaestus was the son of Hera. In some myths, Zeus is named as his father; in others, Hephaestus was fatherless. In either case, Hera wasn't a very good mother; when she saw her newborn son, she was so disgusted by his ugliness that she threw him out of the heavens. Hephaestus fell for nine days and nine nights before he splashed into the ocean, where he was saved by the Oceanids Thetis and Eurynome. For nine years, they hid him in an underwater cave. It was in this cave that Hephaestus learned his craft.

Facing Zeus's Wrath

There's another version of Hephaestus's fall from the heavens: Hephaestus took his mother's side in an argument against Zeus. In a fit of anger, Zeus picked him up by the leg and flung him from Mount Olympus. In this version, Hephaestus fell for just as long, but he landed on the island of Lemnos.

Hephaestus was the god of fire, the smithery, metalworking, and general craftsmanship. He could build just about anything. He never forgot his mother's cruel treatment, and when he was grown, he used his skill to create a beautiful golden throne as a gift to Hera. Dazzled by the magnificent gift, Hera readily accepted it. The moment she sat down, however, the throne trapped her so she couldn't get up again. None of the other deities could figure out how to make the throne release her.

When the gods asked Hephaestus to free his mother, he replied that he had no mother. Eventually, Dionysus got Hephaestus drunk and loaded the smith onto a mule. A procession of Dionysian revelers accompanied the two gods back to Mount Olympus, and Hephaestus told Dionysus how to release Hera.

After this episode, the animosity between Hephaestus and the other Olympians subsided. They accepted him as one of their own, although they still made fun of him from time to time. Hephaestus was ugly and, thanks to his fall from the heavens, also lame. But no one surpassed Hephaestus as a master craftsman, and he built gorgeous halls and palaces on Mount Olympus.

If something could be imagined, Hephaestus could create it. The myths say that he fashioned the first woman from clay. He created the unbreakable chains that bound Prometheus to the mountainside. He made the arrows for Artemis and Apollo, and he also made suits of armor that the other deities gave as gifts to those they favored.

Volcanic Workshops

Many ancients believed that the volcanoes of Sicily and Lemnos held Hephaestus's workshops. So Hephaestus was also considered the god of volcanoes. Some myths say that the Cyclopes, great forgers themselves, worked as Hephaestus's assistants in these volcanic workshops.

Smart, skilled, and generous, Hephaestus's downfall was his unattractive appearance. Despite his impressive talents as a master craftsman, Hephaestus is best known as Aphrodite's husband—and when the myths mention their marriage, they usually point out Aphrodite's infidelity.

HEPHAESTUS AND APHRODITE: AN UNHAPPY UNION

They made an unlikely couple: the goddess of beauty and the ugliest of the gods. Yet these two were husband and wife, although their marriage wasn't a "happily ever after" fairy tale.

After Hephaestus was welcomed to Mount Olympus and accepted as one of the twelve great Olympians, he reconciled with his mother. When Hephaestus saw the beautiful and irresistible goddess of love, he implored his mother to make Aphrodite his wife. Both Hera and Zeus agreed to his request—and they didn't give Aphrodite a choice in the matter. The wedding took place, but the marriage wasn't happy.

As the goddess of love, Aphrodite's nature made her generous in her affections. So it isn't surprising that Aphrodite had numerous affairs outside her marriage. The best-known was with Hephaestus's half-brother, Ares.

Aphrodite loved the one god that everyone else abhorred. They had a passionate love affair, which they kept secret for a time. Eventually, however, their meetings became less discreet. All-seeing Helios discovered their love affair and took the news directly to Hephaestus. Angry and betrayed, Hephaestus decided to get revenge.

He built a great bronze net that only he could handle. He attached the net to the frame of Aphrodite's bed, making sure it was completely hidden. Then he told his wife that he was going on a trip to the island of Lemnos. The moment her husband was gone, Aphrodite invited Ares over.

The lovers went to bed. In the middle of their lovemaking session, the bronze net fell on them. Trapped, naked, and helpless, the lovers could do nothing but wait for Hephaestus to return.

Aphrodite's Cruelty

The goddess of love could punish just as easily as she could bring pleasure. Aphrodite was a dangerous deity. Her punishments were cruel, and even those she favored didn't always fare well. For telling Hephaestus about her affair, Aphrodite made Helios fall in love with the mortal Leucothoe and seduce her. When her father discovered the affair he had his daughter buried alive, and Helios was left to mourn the loss of his love.

When Hephaestus returned, he wasn't alone—he'd brought the other Olympian deities with him to witness the adulterous couple's shameful behavior. The other deities ridiculed Aphrodite and Ares, but they also made fun of Hephaestus, which he hadn't expected.

Poseidon looked at the beautiful, naked, embarrassed Aphrodite and pitied her. He begged Hephaestus to reconcile with his wife and set the couple free. Whether because of Poseidon's intervention or because the Olympians' teasing made Hephaestus feel like a fool, he released the couple.

HERMES

The Messenger—and Prankster—of the Gods

G

Hermes, the messenger of the gods, was charming and likable—if not always well behaved. Mischievous and roguish, Hermes often played tricks to demonstrate his cunning, yet the gods still trusted him with many important missions. A versatile god of many talents, he created inventions that advanced civilization, from numbers to musical instruments, and he was the patron god of diverse groups, including travelers, inventors, liars, thieves, and athletes.

According to one myth, Zeus was enamored with Maia, one of the Pleiades. In order to spend time with her, Zeus had to sneak away from his sleeping wife. One of these meetings led to the birth of Hermes. As Zeus's son, this was no ordinary baby.

Hermes was born at dawn in a cave on Mount Cyllene. By noon, he had developed enough to explore his surroundings and sneak out of the cave. In his explorations, Hermes found a tortoise shell. He used this shell, along with an animal skin and sheep-gut strings, to devise the first lyre. He then taught himself to play the instrument he'd invented—all on the first afternoon of his life.

The Hermaea Festivals

Hermes was born in Arcadia, where he became a popular deity. The Arcadians believed that Hermes was the god of fertility for both humans and animals, and they held festivals in his honor. These festivals, called Hermaea, featured athletic competitions.

TAKE A MESSAGE

Hermes was often in trouble for his mischief. One story explains that Hermes was called before his father to be reprimanded after tricking Apollo. However, Hermes charmed Zeus and convinced him that he would never again tell a lie. The cunning Hermes wanted something in return for his promise: to become Zeus's messenger.

Zeus agreed and gave his son a pair of winged golden sandals, which allowed him to travel with the speed of the wind. He also gave Hermes a wide-brimmed hat and a herald's staff, which became the symbol of his position as messenger of the gods.

As a messenger, Hermes undertook missions on behalf of the other gods and was often entrusted with their secrets and even their welfare. Using his skill and cunning, Hermes usually succeeded in his missions. He even managed to keep his promise to Zeus that he wouldn't lie.

Here are some of Hermes's best-known adventures (but there were many others):

- During Zeus's battle with Typhon, Zeus was left helpless when the monster stole his tendons. Hermes stole the tendons back and replaced them in Zeus's body. This gave Zeus the strength to overcome Typhon.
- After the fifty Danaides (daughters of King Danaus) murdered their husbands, Zeus ordered that they be purified of the murders. Hermes and Athena were responsible for the purifications.
- When Io, Zeus's lover, was changed into a heifer, Hera sent Argus (a hundred-eyed monster) to stand guard over her. To free Io, Zeus sent Hermes to kill Argus. Hermes killed the monster and helped Io to escape.

- Zeus showed Ixion, king of Thessaly, great hospitality and allowed him to sit at the table of the gods on Mount Olympus. But Ixion responded by trying to seduce Hera. This breach of the rules of hospitality was unacceptable, and Zeus ordered Hermes to chain Ixion to an eternally revolving wheel of fire (some myths locate the wheel in the night sky; others put it in Tartarus).
- When Otus and Ephialtes captured Ares and imprisoned him in a bronze jar, it was Hermes who eventually rescued the god of war.
- After the Trojan War, Odysseus's journey home was interrupted by the sea nymph Calypso, who detained him on an island for several years. Calypso wanted Odysseus to become immortal and remain with her forever. Odysseus, however, wanted to go home. Zeus sent Hermes to convince Calypso to let Odysseus leave (which she did, although it broke her heart).
- Upon Zeus's orders, Hermes led Aphrodite, Hera, and Athena to the Trojan prince Paris, who was being raised by a shepherd. The goddesses wanted Paris to settle their dispute about who was the most beautiful.
- Zeus wanted to test mankind and asked Hermes to accompany him to Earth. The two gods wandered the world disguised as travelers. No one offered them hospitality except for one couple, Baucis and Philemon. The gods rewarded these two for their kindness.
- When Dionysus was born, Zeus had to hide him from Hera's wrath. He entrusted his son to Hermes's care.
- Zeus sent Hermes to the Underworld to retrieve Persephone from Hades.

Hermes often came to the aid of the other gods. Although he had a reputation for mischief, the Olympians respected and trusted him, enough to carry their important messages.

MORE THAN A MESSENGER

Hermes's duties went beyond being the deities' messenger. As the protector of travelers, for example, Hermes was said to remove stones from the roads. These stones were often collected and piled around pillars that lined the roads, becoming mini-shrines dedicated to Hermes. In time, these shrines became more elaborate and resembled phalluses, because Hermes was also a fertility god. In fact, several ancient Greek pillars contain carvings that show only the god's face and genitals.

An athletic god, Hermes was associated with athletes and games. He is credited with the invention of boxing, wrestling, and gymnastics. Games were held in Hermes's honor at Pheneus. Gymnasiums were built in his name and displayed his statues. All of the gymnasiums and athletes of Greece were under his protection.

In addition to sports and musical instruments, Hermes took credit for several other inventions. For example, he was said to have worked with the Fates to create the Greek alphabet. The myths also say that he invented astronomy, weights and measures, and the musical scale, and some even say he invented numbers.

Hermes was responsible for guiding the shades of the dead to the Underworld. This important task had previously been undertaken by Hades. Hermes escorted the shades from the upper world to the lower regions as far as the Styx, where Charon ferried them across the river. Hermes was the god who retrieved Persephone from the Underworld. He also escorted Eurydice back into the Underworld when she had almost gained—and then lost—her freedom.

Hermes was the god of eloquence and speech, crops, mining, and buried treasure. He was also the god of prudence, cunning, sleep, fraud, perjury, and theft.

A jack-of-all-trades, Hermes resembled his half brother Apollo in his diverse talents. He also resembled Apollo in physique: Most depictions show Hermes as a handsome, muscular man, usually wearing the winged sandals and hat given to him by Zeus and dressed as a traveler or herald.

A GOD OF MANY MYTHS

Hermes appears in more classical myths than any other deity, often as a supporting character. Because Hermes was so multifaceted, storytellers could easily fit him into their tales: He could be a good guy or a bad guy, a helper or a troublemaker—audiences knew what to expect of him in all of these roles. Hermes could be a messenger, a lover, a helper whose cleverness got the other gods out of fixes, or a mischievous boy who liked to play tricks. Sometimes, his tricks involved stealing from the other gods. He once stole some of Apollo's cattle and later his bow and arrows. Hermes also stole Poseidon's trident, Zeus's scepter, Aphrodite's girdle, and some of Hephaestus's tools. In each case, however, he used his boyish charm to get himself out of trouble. That boyish charm was what made him so popular.

Hermes's personality added a playful touch to Mount Olympus. He was well liked by everyone, mortal and immortal. Often childlike, Hermes could also be responsible and trustworthy when necessary. He performed his duties as a god, but he also had fun. No wonder he appears in so many myths.

SIX WIVES FOR ZEUS

The Original Ladies' Man

G

Although Hera is the best known of Zeus's wives, she was by no means the first. In fact, Zeus had several other wives and lovers before he married Hera. The ruler of the gods had Olympian-size lusts and passions. He was a god who knew what he wanted—and he took what he wanted with little regard for others.

ZEUS'S FIRST WIFE: METIS

Zeus's first wife was Metis, the wise Oceanid who'd advised him to give his father, Cronus, an emetic so he would vomit up Zeus's brothers and sisters. Most myths say that Metis was initially unwilling to succumb to Zeus. She tried to escape his advances by disguising herself, taking on different forms. In the end, Metis grew tired and gave in to Zeus. She became pregnant with a daughter who would become Athena. Metis did not give birth in the traditional sense, however. Zeus swallowed Metis, in order to prevent her from having a son after Athena's birth. When Athena was ready to be born, Zeus had his head split open with an ax, and Athena popped out, fully grown.

Metis, the personification of wisdom, was her husband's equal. Zeus felt a little intimidated by her—and more than a little intimidated by a prophecy that she would be the mother of extremely powerful children who might pose a threat to his power. Zeus dealt with this threat by swallowing Metis, thereby symbolically taking the quality of wisdom into himself.

THEMIS: THE ORDERLY TITANESS

After Metis, Zeus married Themis, one of the original Titanesses and the goddess of necessity and eternal order. Themis worked closely with her husband, acting as his advisor. Together they had several children, including the Moirai (the Fates): Atropus, Clotho, and Lachesis; and the Horae (the Hours): Eunomia (Discipline), Dike (Justice), and Eirene (Peace). The birth of these children completed the order of the universe. Although this marriage also ended, its dissolution wasn't as extreme as Zeus's first divorce; he simply left Themis for another woman.

EURYNOME: MOTHER OF THE GRACES

When Zeus cast his eye upon Eurynome, daughter of Oceanus and Tethys, she was already married to the Titan Ophion. Not only was she married, she was also the sister of Zeus's first wife, Metis. But none of that stopped Zeus. He and Eurynome had three daughters, the Graces: Aglaia (Beauty), Euphrosyne (Joy), and Thalia (Festivity). The Graces brought charm and beauty into the world.

SISTER DEMETER: GODDESS OF AGRICULTURE

Zeus also had a love affair with his sister Demeter, goddess of agriculture and the harvest. Not much is recorded about their relationship.

The myths do record, however, that their union produced a daughter, Persephone.

MNEMOSYNE: MOTHER OF THE MUSES

Zeus's next conquest was Mnemosyne (Memory), a Titaness. Zeus and Mnemosyne made love for nine consecutive nights, leading Mnemosyne to give birth to the nine Muses: Calliope, Clio, Erato, Euterpe, Melpomene, Polyhymnia, Terpsichore, Thalia, and Urania.

LETO: MOTHER OF GREAT OLYMPIAN GODS

Leto, daughter of the Titans Coeus and Phoebe, mated with Zeus and gave birth to the famed twins Apollo and Artemis, who later took their places among the great Olympian gods.

THE WRATH OF HERA

The Most Jealous Goddess of All

G

Zeus was a ladies' man, and had multiple relationships with several goddesses and mortals. Although Zeus's infidelity angered Hera, she tended to take out her feelings on his women instead of him. Granted, most of the women pursued by Zeus tried to escape his advances—but that didn't matter. Hera blamed the women and punished them.

TARGETING IO

One of the best-known stories of Hera's wrath tells of her vengeance upon Io. As you may recall, Zeus seduced Io and then transformed her into a white heifer. This stratagem didn't fool Hera. Pretending to believe Zeus's claims that the heifer was an ordinary cow, she asked him to give her the heifer as a gift. Zeus, who didn't dare refuse his wife, consented and gave Io to Hera. Hera placed the heifer under the guard of Argus, a monster with a hundred eyes.

Zeus felt sorry for Io and sent Hermes to release her. Hermes succeeded in slaying Argus and setting Io free. But that wasn't the end of Io's persecution. Hera found out Io had been released and sent a gadfly to torment the heifer. The gadfly followed Io around, continuously stinging her. Io ran farther and farther away in her attempts to avoid this torment. Eventually, after she'd begged Hera for forgiveness, Io was returned to her true form.

PERSECUTION OF MOTHER AND SON

Another famous story of Hera's wrath is the myth of Alcmene and Heracles. As you know, Hera persuaded her daughter Eileithyia to prevent Alcmene from giving birth to Zeus's child. Heracles was born anyway, making Hera even angrier. She transferred her anger to Heracles.

Hera did everything in her power to punish Heracles, attacking him in many different ways throughout his life. She sent serpents to kill him in his crib, made him a slave, and drove him to madness (which caused him to kill his own wife and children). Throughout all of these torments, Heracles behaved like a hero, so Hera never truly got the better of him. (The life of Heracles contained many exciting adventures.)

THE DEITIES DEBATE

Hera and Zeus once got into a heated debate over who derived the most pleasure from sex: the man or the woman. Zeus claimed that women took greater pleasure in sex, and Hera claimed that men got all the enjoyment. Neither one could convince the other, so they decided to call in Tiresias to settle the dispute.

Tiresias was unusually qualified to judge the matter because he'd lived as both a man and a woman. When he was a child, Tiresias came upon two snakes mating. He took a stick and beat the coupling pair, killing the female. At once, he was transformed into a woman. He lived as a woman for seven years until he chanced upon another pair of mating snakes. This time, he killed the male snake and was transformed back into a man.

When asked his opinion, Tiresias was adamant: Women derive more pleasure from the act of sex. In fact, he said, a woman enjoys lovemaking nine times more than a man does. Hera lost the debate, and she was so furious that she struck Tiresias blind.

MUSES, NYMPHS, SATYRS, AND CHARITES

The Mythical Greats You Need to Know

G

To the ancients, the world was inhabited by thousands of deities and spirits that controlled nature and interacted with humans. Although the Olympians were unquestionably the most powerful deities, a host of other gods appear throughout the myths. They may have been less powerful and less glorious than the mighty Olympians, but these lesser gods played an important role in classical mythology.

THE MUSES: GODDESSES OF THE ARTS

The Muses, daughters of Zeus and Mnemosyne, were the goddesses of music, art, poetry, dance, and the arts in general. These goddesses were honored by the poets and artists who created through their inspiration. Zeus and Mnemosyne made love for nine consecutive nights, creating the nine Muses. Each Muse was in charge of a particular domain of the arts:

- **Calliope:** Epic poetry
- **Clio:** History
- **Erato:** Love poetry, lyric poetry, and marriage songs
- **Euterpe:** Music and lyric poetry

- **Melpomene:** Tragedy
- **Polyhymnia (or Polymnia):** Mime and songs
- **Terpsichore:** Dance
- **Thalia:** Comedy
- **Urania:** Astronomy

The Muses attended celebrations and festivals, singing and dancing for the gods. They were said to be followers of Apollo in his role as the god of music. Although artists invoked the Muses for inspiration, these goddesses had few myths of their own.

Although the Muses were inspirational, they also inflicted punishment. For example, the Pierides (daughters of King Pierus) challenged the Muses to a contest to showcase their own artistic abilities. The Muses were angered by the women's audacity. When the Pierides lost the contest, the Muses turned each of them into a jackdaw (a bird in the crow family). In a similar episode, a bard named Thamyris bragged that he was more skilled than the Muses in the arts of song and poetry. The Muses quickly stifled the man's ego by striking him blind and making him lose his memory.

THE NYMPHS: NATURE'S BEAUTIFUL SPIRITS

Nymphs appear frequently throughout classical mythology. These beautiful nature-goddesses (often, a nymph was the daughter of Zeus or another deity) were eternally youthful. Most nymphs attended upon a higher deity or a higher-ranking nymph. Personifications of fertility and natural grace, they resided in caves, trees, springs, or other bodies of water. The myths relate numerous love affairs involving nymphs and either men or gods. Examples include Poseidon and Amphitrite, Ares and Cyrene, Apollo and Daphne, and Odysseus and Calypso. Different kinds of nymphs could be found throughout nature:

- **Crinaeae:** Lived in fountains
- **Dryads:** Lived in trees
- **Hamadryads:** Lived in specific trees and died when the tree died
- **Leimakids:** Lived in meadows
- **Meliae:** Lived in ash trees
- **Naiads:** Lived in fresh water
- **Napaeae:** Lived in valleys
- **Nereids:** Lived in the sea
- **Oreads:** Lived in mountains
- **Pegaeae:** Lived in springs

Although they were goddesses, the nymphs were not immortal; however, they did live very long lives. Nymphs usually appear as minor characters in myths that feature higher-level gods or heroes. Fun-loving and playful, nymphs were sometimes cruel. For example, if a nymph's beloved refused or mistreated her, she could be vindictive. When the river-nymph Nais discovered her lover's infidelity, she struck him blind. He fell into a river, and the other river-nymphs let him drown.

LUSTY DEITIES: THE SATYRS

The satyrs were nature spirits that personified fertility and sexual desire. Originally they were portrayed as mortal men, but later they came to resemble Pan: with horns, a man's torso and face, and the legs and feet of a goat or, in some myths, a horse.

The satyrs appear in numerous myths, usually as minor characters and often in the company of the great Olympian deities. Satyrs served as comic relief thanks to their mischievous behavior and blatant sexual desire. They were often in drunken, amorous pursuit of nymphs. In the visual arts, satyrs were depicted with enormous, erect penises.

As followers of Dionysus, satyrs participated in the ecstatic Dionysian festivals. They staggered about drunk, playing music and dancing, and trying to quench their lust.

The best-known satyrs were Marsyas and Silenus. Marsyas, as you may recall, challenged Apollo to a musical contest, lost, and paid a terrible price. Silenus was Dionysus's friend and tutor. Known for his wisdom and prophecies, Silenus often overindulged in wine. In fact, he was usually too drunk to walk and had to ride on a donkey instead.

THE CHARITES:
BEAUTY, GRACE, AND FRIENDSHIP

The Charites, also known as the Graces (from their Roman name Gratiae), were minor goddesses of beauty, grace, and friendship (and sometimes charm, nature, creativity, and fertility). The myths disagree on their number and their parentage. Usually, though, there were said to be three Charites, daughters of Zeus and Eurynome.

The most common names for the Charites were Aglaia (Splendor), Euphrosyne (Mirth), and Thalia (Festivity—there was also a Muse named Thalia). These names rose to popularity through Hesiod's

Theogony. Aglaia was said to be the personification of beauty and splendor; Euphrosyne was the personification of joy and merriment; and Thalia personified blossoming and festivity.

The Charites were young, graceful, and beautiful and usually appear in a group. Most commonly seen in art, the Charites in myths are usually in the company of Aphrodite; sometimes they sing and dance in the company of Apollo and the Muses. Like the Muses, the Charites were believed to influence artistic endeavors.

Satyr, ornament on a cast-iron mirror frame, ca. 1900

TRITON, HECATE, AND PAN

Unique Deities, Unique Gifts

G

Although the gods and goddesses of Olympus are considered to be the most important beings in Greek mythology, a comprehensive overview of these great tales would not be complete without mentioning these lesser deities. Triton, Hecate, and Pan, while not as well known as their Olympian predecessors, are still important when discussing Greek mythology, and add color and whimsy to the many stories the ancients told.

TRITON: POSEIDON'S SON

Triton was Poseidon's son and a minor sea deity. Half man, half fish, Triton served as his father's herald and messenger. He possessed powers as well, especially the ability to calm the seas by blowing a conch-shell horn. Triton's conch shell could also instill fear. For example, during the war between the Giants and the Olympians, the loud blasts from Triton's conch shell frightened the Giants; they ran away, thinking that the sound came from a monster. Like his father, Triton carried a trident.

Triton appears in several myths. He was the father of Pallas, Athena's young playmate whom she accidentally killed. Another myth tells of the assistance Triton gave to the Argonauts. During the quest for the Golden Fleece, a huge tidal wave carried the *Argo* inland, and the Argonauts found themselves on Lake Tritonis. (Some myths say the wave carried them into the desert of Libya.) For days, the Argonauts searched for a way to return to the sea, but to no avail.

Disguised as a mortal named Eurypylus, Triton introduced himself to the Argonauts, who welcomed him with great hospitality. To show his appreciation for their kindness, he showed the men a route that would return them to the sea. Some myths say that Triton pushed the ship along the land, all the way back to the sea.

Triton wasn't always honorable. Like most gods, he had a complex character. According to one myth, during a festival held in honor of Dionysus, Triton came upon some women bathing in the sea in preparation for the rites. Unable to restrain his lust, Triton harassed the women, who called upon Dionysus for help. The god of the vine rushed to their aid, and the two gods fought. Triton lost.

Another myth shows Triton as a thief who stole cattle and attacked ships. To stop him, the local people left out a bowl filled with wine. Triton found the wine and drank it all, and then passed out. As he slept, someone (some say Dionysus) beheaded him with an ax.

A Magical Island

Triton gave one Argonaut, Euphemus, a clod of earth. Shortly after the *Argo* had passed the island of Crete, Euphemus dropped the clod of earth into the sea. At the place where it landed, the island of Calliste sprang up.

HECATE:
TITANESS WITH AN ATTITUDE

After the Olympians defeated the Titans, most of the Titans were sent to Tartarus. A few, however, were spared this eternal torture because they'd refused to fight against Zeus; Hecate was one of these. After the war, she was able to keep her powers over earth, sky, and sea (although her powers in these realms were inferior to Zeus's).

Early myths show Hecate as a benevolent goddess associated with the Earth, like Demeter. Hecate oversaw the soil's fertility, ensuring that crops could grow. After the fall of the Titans, her powers became more numerous: She could grant eloquence in speech to orators, material prosperity to any mortal, and victory in battle to warriors. As a goddess of prosperity, she could grant bountiful catches to fishermen and fertile livestock to farmers. Mortals often looked to Hecate for help and blessings, and she was easily persuaded to grant favors.

Shifting to the Darker Side

Later, Hecate's character underwent a gradual change, growing darker and more menacing. Hecate transformed from a benevolent earth goddess to a goddess of sorcery and witchcraft. Later myths show her as a goddess of the night, associated with the land of the dead. Some myths say she was an attendant and confidante of Persephone, Queen of the Underworld. Although a virgin goddess, Hecate was associated with childbirth and rearing. She was also associated with gates and doorways, the moon, torches, dogs, ghosts, magic and witchcraft, and curses. Worshipers built shrines to Hecate at crossroads because these spots were associated with magical rites.

Ghoulish Happenings

Hecate was said to haunt graveyards. At night, she would walk among the graves with her dogs, searching for souls not yet transported to the Underworld. If a black dog was seen in a graveyard, people believed that Hecate would soon appear.

Hecate sometimes appears in art as a woman with three faces. Usually, she carries torches and has a pack of hellhounds baying at her side.

The Importance of Three

The number three was associated with Hecate, who was considered a triple goddess. Her three faces, looking in three different directions, could see past, present, and future. Similarly, she had control over the three phases of existence: birth, life, and death. She had three sacred emblems: a key, a dagger, and a rope. Hecate was also said to appear at crossroads where a traveler faced three choices.

Hecate had different names to indicate the different facets of her character. Here are a few of them:

- **Apotropaia:** Protector
- **Chthonia:** Of the Underworld
- **Kourotrophos:** Nurse
- **Propolos:** Attendant
- **Trimorphe:** Three-formed
- **Trioditis:** Of three roads

Although a minor goddess, Hecate was powerful and influential in the classical mythology. Today, she is still invoked by those interested in witchcraft and magic.

PAN: THE GOD OF WOODS AND PASTURES

Son of Hermes and the god of shepherds and flocks, Pan was half man and half goat. When he was born, his mother was so frightened at the sight of her child that she ran away, taking the nurse with her. But Hermes was proud of his son and introduced him to the Olympians.

It is easy to see why Pan's mother was horrified. In art, Pan is shown with two horns on his forehead and with the ears, tail, legs, and hooves of a goat. The young god was raised by nymphs and became a mountain dweller. His physical characteristics made it easy for him to climb rocks and move quickly over the rough terrain.

As a woodland god, Pan was worshiped primarily in rural areas. He was believed to be responsible for the fertility of animals. When a herd's animals did not reproduce, Pan was blamed for their barrenness, and his statues were defaced. (Most gods would erupt with anger over such treatment, but it didn't bother Pan. He grew much angrier if his sleep was interrupted.)

As a fertility god—one whose lower half took the form of an animal renowned for its lust—Pan was famous for his sexual ability and was frequently shown with an erect phallus. He often chased nymphs, trying to catch and violate them. One such nymph was Syrinx.

A follower of Artemis, Syrinx did not want to have sex with Pan and tried to outrun him, but Pan was very fast. He chased her to a river's edge. Trapped, unable to cross the river, Syrinx begged the river nymphs to save her. They granted her wish, transforming her into a bed of reeds, just as Pan reached the scene.

Disappointed, Pan breathed a huge sigh. His breath blew through the hollow reeds and made a delightful, musical sound. Pan cut several different lengths of the reeds and tied them together to make a set of pipes. This instrument became known as panpipes, or syringes.

OTHER LESSER GODS

The Powerful Beings You Should Know

G

As you read about Greek mythology, you're likely to come across a number of other minor deities. Here are a few you should know about.

- **Boreas:** The North Wind. Boreas was often depicted as violent and untrustworthy. Like many other gods, he sometimes abducted and raped mortal women.
- **Eris:** Goddess of discord and strife. She often accompanied Ares on the battlefield. Eris was the source of the golden apple that created conflict among Aphrodite, Athena, and Hera and ultimately led to the Trojan War.
- **Eros:** God of love, particularly sensual love. Eros is often depicted as carrying a bow and arrows; his gold-tipped arrows inspired love, whereas his lead-tipped arrows caused hatred or, at best, indifference. Sometimes, because love is blind, this god was shown blindfolded.
- **Eurus:** The East Wind. He was usually described as being wet and blustery.
- **The Fates:** Three goddesses in charge of determining a person's lifespan. These goddesses spun, measured, and cut each individual's thread of life. Some myths say that they could also determine whether a person would be good or evil. Everyone—even the Olympians—was subject to the Fates.

- **Hebe:** Goddess of youth. Daughter of Zeus and Hera, Hebe was the cupbearer to the gods for a time. Later, she became the wife of Heracles when he joined the deities on Mount Olympus.
- **Hymen:** God of marriage. He was normally shown leading a wedding procession.
- **Iris:** Goddess of the rainbow, which connected the sky and Earth. Iris was also a messenger of the gods.
- **Nemesis:** Goddess of vengeance. She was usually called upon to avenge those who had been wronged, but she was also in charge of limiting excess. If someone became too rich or had an unending streak of good luck, for example, Nemesis would take away some of that person's good fortune, to keep the universe in balance.
- **Nike:** Goddess of victory. Often seen in the company of Zeus, Nike also visited conquerors and victors; she would hold a crown of victory above their heads.
- **Notus:** The South Wind. He was normally associated with the warmth and moistness of a gentle wind. In the autumn, however, Notus was thought to turn angry and bring storms that destroyed crops.
- **Thanatos:** God of death. Thanatos was the twin brother of Hypnos, god of sleep. When a person's thread of life had run short, Thanatos would visit that mortal and cut off a lock of his or her hair. When Thanatos had snipped your hair, there was no going back: You were dedicated to Hades.
- **Tyche:** Goddess of fortune and the personification of luck. She was one of the Oceanids.
- **Zephyrus:** The West Wind. Zephyrus, the god of spring breezes, was considered the gentlest of all of the wind gods. However, one myth blames Zephyrus for the death of Hyacinthus, so this god also had his violent side.

In addition to the great gods whose power resounded throughout the universe, every hill, every river, every spring, even every individual tree seemed to have its own god or goddess. This conception of the world makes the universe seem both ordered and chaotic: ordered because each deity has his or her domain, but chaotic because the desires of those many gods sometimes came into conflict.

MYTHS IN MOVIES AND POPULAR CULTURE

Bring the Magic of the Myths to the Big Screen

G R

Filmmakers are always in search of compelling stories to bring to the big screen. With the variety of subjects, themes, and plots offered within classical mythology, it's surprising that few movies adhere closely to mythological storylines. Many films make allusions to mythology, but few tell the actual stories.

In 1956, director Robert Wise released *Helen of Troy*, an ambitious attempt to depict the events of the Trojan War. This lavish spectacle tried to be as authentic as possible. The film focuses on Helen (Rossana Podesta) and her love affair with Paris (Jacques Sernas) in the context of the Trojan War.

A more recent cinematic depiction of the Trojan War is *Troy* (2004), directed by Wolfgang Petersen. A star-studded cast was led by Brad Pitt (Achilles), Eric Bana (Hector), Diane Kruger (Helen), Orlando Bloom (Paris), and Peter O'Toole (Priam). The film uses the *Iliad*, the *Aeneid*, and other ancient texts as its sources, but the film departs from those sources in many ways. For example, it leaves out the judgment of Paris as the starting point of the conflict and does not show the gods and goddesses as active participants. Some characters who survived the war in the ancient myths get killed during battle on screen, including Menelaus and Agamemnon.

Other movies based on the stories of classical mythology include these:

- *Orpheus* (1949), directed by Jean Cocteau
- *Ulysses* (1955), directed by Mario Camerini
- *Hercules* (1957), directed by Pietro Francisci
- *Jason and the Argonauts* (1963), directed by Don Chaffey
- *Clash of the Titans* (1981), directed by Desmond Davis
- *Mighty Aphrodite* (1995), directed by Woody Allen
- *O Brother, Where Art Thou?* (2000), directed by Ethan Coen and Joel Coen
- *Clash of the Titans* (2010), directed by Louis Leterrier (remake of the 1981 film)

MYTHS IN POPULAR CULTURE

Mythology doesn't belong exclusively to the world of "high art." It's appeared in television shows, cartoons, comic books, toys, and video games. In myths, the stories are action-packed, the monsters terrifying, and the heroes larger than life.

From 1995 through 1999, *Hercules: The Legendary Journeys* was a popular television series loosely based on myths of Heracles, his labors, and his adventures. Kevin Sorbo played Hercules, and the series spun off action figures and other memorabilia. Its most popular spinoff was another television series *Xena: Warrior Princess*, which ran between 1995 and 2001. Xena, played by Lucy Lawless, wasn't a mythological figure, but she represented an Amazon-like female warrior.

Another popular spinoff featuring Hercules and Xena was the full-length animated film *Hercules & Xena: The Battle for Olympus* (1997). In this film, voiced by the television shows' actors, Hercules and Xena team up to overcome the Titans, who've been freed by Hera in a bid to become ruler of the universe.

The year 1997 also saw the release of Walt Disney Pictures' animated film *Hercules*. Although somewhat watered down for its young audience, the film kept the essence of the Heracles myths portraying the hero as a man who, through his ambition and accomplishments, achieved the highest reward: immortality.

Even Disney Shares the Myths

Disney's early animated film *Fantasia* (1940) features characters from Greek mythology that range from Centaurs to Zeus.

Comic books also depict mythological themes and characters. Marvel Comics featured the adventures of Zeus beginning in 1940. Selene, whose name comes from the ancient moon goddess, is a villainess in Marvel's *X-Men* comic books. In the world of DC Comics, Wonder Woman is a modern version of an Amazon, and one of her main enemies is named Circe. The Erinyes (Furies) appear in several volumes of DC Comics' *Sandman* series.

Want to live the life of an ancient hero? Video games put you right in the middle of the action. *God of War*, for PlayStation 2, is an award-winning video game whose main character, Kratos, is sent on a quest by Athena to kill Ares. Other games in this popular series include *God of War II* (2007), *God of War: Chains of Olympus* (2008), and *God of War III* (2010). Gamers with a taste for mythology can also try *Age of Mythology* (2002), *Titan Quest* (2006), and *Rise of the Argonauts* (2008).

SCYLLA

From Gorgeous Nymph to Repulsive Monster

G

Unlike other monsters, Scylla wasn't born hideous. She began her life a beautiful sea nymph, happy and carefree. Scylla enjoyed the company of the other sea nymphs, but she did not share their enthusiasm for lust and love. In fact, she wanted nothing to do with men and lovemaking. She was happy as she was and rejected all suitors—until she caught the attention of Glaucus.

Glaucus was a sea deity who fell in love with the beautiful Scylla. He knew she disliked men, and he also knew he'd need the help of magic to have his way with her. Glaucus went to the witch Circe and asked her to create a love potion that would leave Scylla helpless against him, but his plan backfired.

Who Was Circe?

Circe was the daughter of Helios. She was a powerful witch who almost always used her powers for evil. For example, she turned her enemies into animals and was especially cruel to those who rejected her love. (Circe appears in the *Odyssey*, a classic mythological text.)

Circe fell in love with Glaucus, but Glaucus cared for no one but Scylla. When Circe declared her love for Glaucus, he rejected her. Furious, Circe decided to take her rival out of the running. She concocted a potion of poisonous herbs and added it to Scylla's bathwater.

Different myths describe the potion's effect in different ways. One myth says that it transformed Scylla only from the waist down, affecting the part of her body that was submerged in the water. Scylla's upper body remained that of a beautiful woman, but her lower body was hideously changed: The heads of six vicious dogs encircled her waist. These dogs, constantly barking and hungry for prey, would attack anything that got close to Scylla.

In another account, Scylla's entire body was transformed so that no trace of her former beauty remained. Scylla now had six heads (each with three rows of teeth) and twelve feet. Now, Scylla inspired fear in all who saw her.

The monstrous Scylla made her home by the sea between Italy and Sicily, where she lived in a cave next to the whirlpool of Charybdis. There, Scylla waited for sailors to pass. Ships trying to navigate the strait had to maneuver to avoid the whirlpool. This caused the ship to sail closer to the rocky cliffs where Scylla lurked in her cave. While the sailors were preoccupied with avoiding the whirlpool, Scylla would strike, snatching as many men as she could from the deck of the ship and devouring them.

The Terrors of Charybdis

Charybdis was merciless. Sailors knew to avoid its whirlpool at all costs, for to approach too near meant certain destruction. Three times a day, the whirlpool sucked in everything in the waters that surrounded it. Then three times a day, the whirlpool spewed out the seawater and objects it had consumed earlier. So sailors navigating the strait had to avoid being sucked into the whirlpool, and at the same time, they had to avoid the disgorged flotsam.

AMAZONS

Fierce Women, Incredible Warriors

G

According to one myth, Ares, the god of war, mated with an Amazon queen, and their union produced another Amazon queen. Ares was an important god to the entire Amazon race, not just those who were looking for help in battle. The myths surrounding these women were popular in ancient times.

The Amazons were a mythological nation of female warriors. They were thought to have their own laws, their own means of providing food and shelter, and their own government ruled by a queen. Different myths site the Amazons' realm in different locations, including Thrace, Scythia, the Caucasus Mountains, and the areas occupied by modern-day Turkey or Libya.

THE MEN AND CHILDREN

According to the myths, Amazon women could not bear to be in the presence of a man. (The only exceptions were male servants who performed menial tasks.) Of course, the Amazons also needed men to propagate their race. So Amazon women mated with strangers, normally travelers or foreigners, with the intention of getting pregnant. These women wanted nothing more to do with the biological fathers of their children. There was no such thing as a father in Amazon culture.

When a male child was born, the Amazons disposed of the baby. Some stories say the Amazons sent male children to live with their fathers. Others paint the Amazons as cruel, injuring the child in some way (perhaps by blinding) and then leaving him to die. (Occasionally, a kind passerby took pity on the wounded child.) Yet others say the male babies were killed at birth. A few male children, however, were allowed to live and raised as slaves of the tribe.

Girl children were valued. Yet because the girls were destined to become warriors, they were raised with that outcome in mind. Since the right breast could interfere with a woman's skill in archery, the girls were fed mare's milk to prevent them from developing breasts, according to some myths. Other myths say that the Amazons cut off or burned the girls' right breasts to ensure their skill. Classical writers have also traced the word *Amazon* to *a-mazos*, which meant "without a breast."

WARRIOR PRINCESSES

Like Ares, the Amazons revered war. War was their passion and their talent. They worshiped Ares, whom they considered the father of their tribe, and his half sister Artemis, a virgin goddess who represented female strength and shunned men.

Several Greek heroes—such as Heracles, Bellerophon, and Theseus—appear in myths with the Amazons. The Amazons were also featured in the Trojan War. They fought on the side of the Trojans, and their queen, Penthesilea, was killed by Achilles.

SUPERWOMEN

In art, Amazon women were depicted like the male warriors of the time. Normally seen on horseback, the Amazons wore armor made of animal skins and carried either a bow or spear. An Amazon warrior possessed the strength of a man and was as savage as a wild animal, but she was especially dangerous because she had reason and cunning.

Portraying the Amazonomachy

The Amazons were a favorite subject of Greek art, which usually depicted the Amazonomachy. This battle between the Greeks and the Amazons appears in all kinds of ancient Greek art, including pottery and sculpture.

The myths about the Amazons entertained men and women alike, but in different ways. Ancient Greece was essentially a man's world in which women had few rights, so the Amazons, a symbol of freedom and strength, were admired by many housewives of the time. (These women probably enjoyed the stories about the Amazons having male servants to do household chores.) The men, on the other hand, were in awe of the Amazons. The idea that a woman did not need men, that she could possess the same strength as a man (or perhaps even greater), must have been a bit frightening. For the ancients, the figure of the Amazon held both horror and fascination.

MINOTAUR

An A-Maze-Ingly Terrifying Monster

Ⓖ

The creation of the Minotaur can be traced back to the conflict between King Minos of Crete and Poseidon over the sacrifice of a beautiful bull. Poseidon had sent the bull to Minos, expecting the king to sacrifice the animal in his honor. But Minos was so enthralled by the bull's beauty that he refused to go through with the sacrifice. The king's wife, Pasiphae, was also taken with the bull; in fact, she fell in love with it. (Some myths claim that Poseidon made Pasiphae fall in love with the bull to get back at Minos for denying the god his sacrifice.)

Pasiphae was consumed by physical desire for the bull; she ordered the craftsman Daedalus to build a hollowed-out cow form. She hid herself within this form and was mounted by the beautiful bull. Pasiphae conceived a child through this union; her son was called Minotaur.

The Minotaur was a monster with the body of a man and the head of a bull. Pasiphae suckled the creature when it was a baby, but it grew into a ferocious, maneating monster. Not quite sure what to do with this creature, Minos consulted the oracle at Delphi, and then ordered Daedalus to construct an extremely complicated maze, or labyrinth.

The labyrinth that Daedalus built was so intricate that no one who entered was able to find the way out. The labyrinth became the Minotaur's prison. Shut away in this maze, the Minotaur wandered its passageways, killing and eating any living creature it found.

Minos made a name for himself as a conqueror of many lands. He declared himself ruler of the seas and was in constant pursuit of new territory. He made war on Athens because his son Androgeus had died there. But Athens was too well defended, and Minos's army was unable to take the city. So Minos changed tactics. He prayed for a great plague to sweep over Athens. (Since Minos was the son of Zeus, his prayers were usually well received.)

The gods answered his prayers, and Athens was struck with a pestilence so fierce that King Aegeus was forced to bargain with Minos. Minos said that he would ask the gods to lift the plague if King Aegeus would send him a tribute of fourteen youths: seven men and seven maidens. (Some myths say the tribute was to be sent every year; some myths say every nine years.) Aegeus consulted the Delphic oracle and learned that this was the only way to end the plague. He agreed to the tribute Minos demanded.

At the appointed time, Athens sent seven young men and seven young women to Crete. Their fate was to become food for the Minotaur; they were thrown into the labyrinth, where they were trapped until the Minotaur found and devoured them. Entering the labyrinth meant certain death at the hands of a terrifying, merciless monster.

Aegeus's Tragic End

When Theseus sailed for Crete, he told his father that he would unfurl a white sail on his journey home if he was successful in his quest to kill the Minotaur. If he was killed, however, the ship would use black sails. On his journey home, Theseus forgot to unfurl the white sail. King Aegeus, watching for a white sail, believed that Theseus had been killed and, in his grief, hurled himself into the sea.

Twice, Athens sent young people to Crete to be sacrificed to the Minotaur. When it was time for the third tribute, Theseus, King Aegeus's son, volunteered to go so that he could kill the Minotaur and end the slaughter of young Athenians. When he arrived in Crete, Theseus won the love of Ariadne, Minos's daughter, and she taught him how to escape the labyrinth: There was one path to the center, where the Minotaur dwelled. Ariadne gave Theseus a ball of thread, so he could unwind it as he made his way through the labyrinth and then retrace his path to the entrance. Theseus killed the Minotaur with his father's sword and led the other Athenians out of the maze, following the thread.

Minotaur, from a Corinthian amphora, fifth century B.C.

CHIMERA

The Merciless, Fire-Breathing, Nightmare-Inducing Creature

G

The Chimera was the monstrous daughter of Typhon and Echidna. She breathed fire and had the head of a lion (Hesiod said she had three heads), the body of a goat, and the tail of a snake. This monster terrorized the people of Lycia and was defeated by the hero Bellerophon.

A mortal, Bellerophon was famous for having tamed Pegasus, a winged horse. Bellerophon accidentally killed his brother (although some myths say the victim wasn't his brother at all, but a tyrant) and was exiled from his homeland. He went to Argos to be purified. There, King Proetus welcomed Bellerophon into his kingdom and purified him of the murder.

Things were going well for the young man until the king's wife fell in love with him. He refused her advances; in retaliation, she falsely accused him of attempted rape. King Proetus was torn: He couldn't let such a crime against his wife go unpunished, but he liked the young man. Besides, Bellerophon was a guest in his home, and he would be breaking the laws of hospitality if he put his guest to death. Proetus decided to send Bellerophon to his father-in-law's kingdom with a sealed letter ordering his execution.

Ignorant of the contents of the letter, Bellerophon left Argos and made his way to Lycia. King Iobates greeted him warmly and entertained his guest for a week before he remembered the letter. When the king opened the letter and saw what it demanded, he found himself in the same predicament as Proetus. He had accepted Bellerophon as a guest in his home, and he didn't want the young man's blood on his hands. Instead of executing Bellerophon, the king ordered him to kill the Chimera, which had been terrorizing his kingdom.

The king was sure that Bellerophon would be killed in this quest; no one could stand up to the Chimera. The monster was merciless and destroyed everything in her path. No single person could withstand it.

But Bellerophon wasn't an ordinary person. He had tamed Pegasus, so he had an ally in the battle. The Chimera's fire-breath was her most deadly weapon, and Pegasus flew Bellerophon out of range. The hero swooped down on the Chimera, showering her with arrows. According to one version of this myth, Bellerophon attached a block of lead to the end of his spear. He managed to thrust the lead into the Chimera's throat, where her fiery breath melted it, causing her to suffocate. Bellerophon returned to King Iobates with news of his triumph.

Chimera, from an Etruscan bronze, fifth century B.C.

MEDUSA

The Witch with a Bad Hair Day

Ⓖ

Medusa is one of the most famous creatures in Greek mythology. She was a Gorgon: one of three monstrous sisters that had serpents for hair (like the Erinyes), claws, and long, sharp teeth. Some say they had wings and impenetrable scales covering their bodies. Looking at a Gorgon would turn any being to stone. Medusa was the most famous of the Gorgons.

Despite this hellish appearance, some myths explain that Medusa wasn't always a terrifying, hideous creature. In these myths, she was once a beautiful woman, and her beauty attracted Poseidon's attention.

One day, when Medusa was visiting one of Athena's temples, Poseidon approached her, expressing his desire. They made love in the temple—an unacceptable and forbidden act to the virgin goddess Athena. Furious at her disobedience, Athena turned Medusa into the horrifying monster she is known as today. However, this punitive transformation wasn't enough for Athena. Later, Athena helped Perseus to slay Medusa, unleashing her full wrath and vengeance.

A Grotesque Son for Medusa

Cacus was the son of Hephaestus and Medusa. Inheriting the properties of fire from his father and monstrousness from his mother, Cacus was a fire-breathing monster who was sometimes described as a three-headed giant. He lived on human flesh and decorated his cave with the bones and skulls of his victims.

PERSEUS: MEDUSA'S BANE

Perseus, another great hero from ancient Greece, accepted a mission from King Polydectes to retrieve Medusa's head. With her monstrous size and a stare that could turn mortals and immortals alike to stone, obtaining Medusa's head seemed an impossible task. However, Perseus knew with the goddess Athena on his side, he would be victorious.

Athena had her own reasons for wanting Perseus to succeed. To put it simply, she hated Medusa, and wanted revenge for her tryst with Poseidon in the temple. Athena gave Perseus a polished bronze shield and offered him guidance, and Perseus readily accepted.

When Perseus reached Medusa's lair, Athena told him what to do. Instead of looking at the sleeping Medusa directly—which would turn him to stone—Perseus watched her reflection in his bronze shield. Keeping his eyes on the reflection, rather than looking at Medusa herself, Perseus beheaded the monster.

Perseus knew that he never would have succeeded without Athena, so he showed his appreciation by mounting Medusa's head on Athena's shield. A Gorgon's head was a great aid in battle, because it had the power to paralyze one's enemies. This shield became a symbol of the goddess, and rarely was she depicted without it.

Trust in Athena

Some myths say that Perseus didn't have to rely on the reflection in the bronze shield to defeat Medusa. He simply kept his eyes shut and trusted Athena to guide his sword, knowing that her hatred of Medusa would not fail him.

Two children appeared when Perseus sliced off Medusa's head—Chrysaor and Pegasus—the results of her union with Poseidon. One myth says that both were born when drops of Medusa's blood landed in the sea. Some myths say that Pegasus was born from her blood, and Chrysaor was born from her neck.

Medusa, from a sixth-century B.C. vase

CENTAURS

Depraved Equestrians You Should Fear

G

The Centaurs were a race of beings that had the head and torso of a man and the body and legs of a horse. With a few notable exceptions, the race was brutal and savage. Centaurs enjoyed devouring raw flesh and were constantly on the hunt for it. Usually violent and looking for a fight, Centaurs represented savagery and uncivilized life. Caught between the human and animal world, their human side couldn't overcome their wild animal nature.

The most famous myth involving the Centaurs tells of their battle with the Lapithae, people who lived in Thessaly. Pirithous, the Lapith king, invited the Centaurs to his wedding. All went well until the Centaurs got drunk and began trying to rape the women, including the bride. A great fight broke out between the Centaurs and the Lapithae, with casualties on both sides. Eventually, the Lapithae drove out the Centaurs. Both the *Iliad* and the *Odyssey* refer to this fight, which was also a frequent subject in ancient Greek art.

Centaur, battling a dragon, from a stone boss, Westminster Abbey, London, ca. 1250–58

MORE MONSTERS: GRIFFINS, ERINYES, HARPIES, AND THE HYDRA OF LERNA

The Original Creatures That Go Bump in the Night

G

Myths tell larger-than-life stories of heroes and explore primal fears. So it's not surprising that they're populated by monsters. You have already read about a few of the better-known monsters, but as you read the myths, you're sure to encounter others. Here are some of the monsters you might meet.

- **Griffins:** These monsters guarded treasure and were often employed by the gods and goddesses. A griffin had the head and wings of an eagle and the body of a lion. When these creatures were on guard, a treasure was almost always protected.

- **Erinyes:** Also known by their Roman name, the Furies, the Erinyes were born from drops of blood when Cronus threw his father's severed genitals into the sea. The Erinyes had snakes for hair, their eyes dripped blood, and their bodies looked like winged dogs. Their name means "angry ones," and it was their job to torment people who broke the laws of nature. In the *Oresteia*, the Erinyes pursue Orestes for murdering his mother, until Athena intervenes.

- **Harpies:** Harpies were birds with women's faces. Fierce creatures with sharp claws, they were often sent by the deities to punish criminals. When anything was missing—including children—the Harpies were thought to be responsible.
- **Hydra of Lerna:** The Hydra was a giant serpent with numerous heads and poisonous breath; different myths say that this monster had anywhere from five to a hundred heads. Whenever one head was cut off, two more grew in its place. The Hydra fought against Heracles, aided by a giant crab.

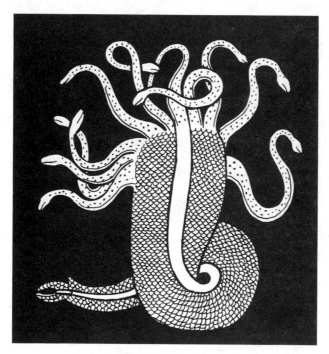

Hydra, as depicted on a vase

Griffin, from a late medieval drawing

SPHINX

Master of Riddles, Eater of Man

G

The Sphinx was another monstrous daughter of Typhon and Echidna. She had the head and breasts of a woman, the body of a lion, and the wings of a bird of prey. A vicious, maneating monster, the Sphinx enjoyed playing with her food like a cat toying with a mouse. Her favorite game offered her victims a riddle to solve. If the victim could solve the riddle, the Sphinx promised to let the person go. Although many tried, they all failed and were devoured.

The Sphinx lived in the mountains outside Thebes, where she harassed travelers and residents of the city. Oedipus, traveling to Thebes, encountered the Sphinx, who stopped him and demanded that he try to answer her riddle: "What creature walks on four legs in the morning, two at noon, and three in the evening?"

Unlike those who'd tried and failed to answer this puzzling riddle, Oedipus answered, "Man." In the "morning" of life (that is, in infancy), a baby crawls on all fours; at "noon," or the prime of life, a person walks upright on two legs; in the "evening" of life, an old person relies on a cane.

Oedipus gave the correct answer. The Sphinx was so shocked and furious that she threw herself off a cliff. The city of Thebes was saved. In gratitude, the people made Oedipus their king and gave him the hand of Jocasta, the recently widowed queen.

WHAT MAKES A HERO?

Ancient Legends with Modern Connections

G

Today, people use the word *hero* to describe any person who does something brave or admirable. The ancients, however, had different ideas about what makes a hero—and bravery was just the beginning. Heroes had to satisfy a long list of requirements, some of which modern people would find surprising. Here, you'll find out what heroism meant to the ancients, and how heroes impacted some of classical mythology's most popular stories.

HEROISM — GREEK STYLE

When you think of a hero, you probably imagine someone who risks his or her own interests—or even life—to help someone else. Today, a hero can be anyone who acts with courage or integrity. Most people would say that heroism is defined more by how a person acts than by whom that person is.

The ancient Greeks would agree with some parts of that definition but would scratch their heads at others. To the ancients, a hero had to be a certain kind of person and act in a certain way. Here are some of the qualities that defined a hero:

- **Noble:** Heroes were of high birth. Often, at least one parent was divine.
- **Courageous:** Heroes didn't show fear in the face of a challenge.

- **Strong:** Heroes possessed great physical strength—in some cases, to an almost supernatural degree.
- **Bold:** Without hesitation, heroes undertook difficult quests, adventures, and exploits to prove themselves.
- **Skillful:** Often the skill mastered by heroes was warfare, but they were expected to excel in some pursuit.
- **Hospitable:** The laws of hospitality were important to the ancients, and heroes were expected to follow them, whether as host or as guest.
- **Favored by the gods:** The gods took an interest in heroes—sometimes opposing them and sometimes supporting them. But usually a hero had at least one powerful god on his side.

Heroes often performed amazing feats that no ordinary person could accomplish. They were mortal, and they were rewarded by the gods after death. Heroes also had very human flaws, such as pride, rage, or jealousy. Unlike modern heroes, classical heroes could be self-centered; they were concerned with their reputation and sometimes put themselves ahead of others. Finally, heroes had to be able to help their friends (showing loyalty) and hurt their enemies (showing bravery and fierceness).

THE TWELVE LABORS OF HERACLES

Heracles: Greece's Most Famous Hero

G

Heracles is probably the most famous hero of Greek mythology. He is so prominent in the myths that previous chapters have already mentioned him several times; it's impossible to talk about some of the gods or monsters without mentioning Heracles. He was a hero who gained immortality by shedding blood, sweat, and tears.

Son of a Mortal and a God

Heracles was the son of Zeus and Alcmene, a mortal woman. At birth, he was given the name Alcides. In order to pacify jealous Hera, who persecuted the boy mercilessly, he was renamed Heracles, or "glory of Hera." The new name didn't mollify Hera one bit, and she continued to vex Heracles.

HOME TO THEBES

On his way back to Thebes, his native city, Heracles ran into a group of men sent from the ruling Minyans to collect the annual tribute of one hundred cattle from the defeated Thebans. He cut off their ears, noses, and hands and tied the severed parts around their necks. He sent them back to their king with the message that Thebes was no longer under his control.

Of course, the Minyans retaliated, but due to Heracles's skill in warfare, Thebes was ready. Heracles gathered an army of Thebans and attacked the Minyan city. The Thebans won the war, and in gratitude, the king of Thebes gave Heracles his daughter Megara in marriage.

Megara and Heracles had three sons and lived happily together—until Hera found them. Hera hadn't given up her quest to destroy Zeus's illegitimate son and struck Heracles with a fit of madness. Heracles murdered his three sons and Megara, who had tried to shield one of her sons with her body. Next, Heracles tried to kill his foster father Amphitryon, but Athena hit Heracles with a rock and knocked him unconscious. When the young man came to, he was horrified to realize what he had done.

To purify himself and purge his guilt for murdering his family, Heracles consulted the Delphic oracle, which ordered him to go to King Eurystheus of Tiryns and there accomplish ten tasks given to him by the king. Successfully completing these tasks would purify Heracles and give him immortality so that he could take his place among the gods. More anxious to atone for his sins than for immortality, Heracles complied.

A True Ancient Hero

According to one myth, two nymphs visited Heracles when he was a young man. The nymphs, named Pleasure and Virtue, offered Heracles a choice: He could have either a comfortable, easy life or a difficult, glorious life—but not both. Like a true hero, Heracles chose hardship and glory.

THE TWELVE LABORS

Although the oracle specified that Heracles must complete ten tasks, Eurystheus judged that he had not successfully completed two of them. Heracles had twice received aid, so he did not complete those two labors on his own. So Eurystheus created two more labors, bringing the total to twelve:

1. **Kill the Nemean Lion.** This lion had a hide so thick that arrows and spears could not pierce it. Heracles had to fight the lion with his bare hands. Thanks to his incredible strength, he was able to wrestle the lion to the ground and strangle it.
2. **Kill the Hydra of Lerna.** The Hydra was a great serpent with many heads. Heracles attacked the monster, but each time he cut off one head, two more grew in its place. He had to call on his nephew Iolaus for help. When Heracles chopped off a head, Iolaus cauterized the stump, preventing new heads from growing. The Hydra had one immortal head, which Heracles buried under a rock. Although Heracles defeated the Hydra, Eurystheus deemed that he hadn't completed this task successfully because he'd had assistance.
3. **Capture the Cerynitian Hind.** This deer with golden antlers was sacred to Artemis. To avoid offending that goddess, Heracles had to capture it unharmed. He hunted the hind for a full year and finally caught it in a net as it slept.
4. **Capture the Erymanthian Boar.** For years, a vicious boar had plagued the countryside of Psophis. Heracles stood outside the boar's lair and shouted loudly. The boar ran out of the lair, straight into a snowdrift. Heracles caught the boar in chains and took it back to Eurystheus.

5. **Clean the Augean Stables.** Heracles's first four tasks had brought him glory; the fifth was intended to be both humiliating and impossible. These stables, which belonged to King Augeas, were home to thousands of cattle and hadn't been cleaned in thirty years. Heracles was charged with cleaning the stables in a single day. To accomplish this task, Heracles diverted the courses of two rivers to make them run through the stables. The rivers washed away all the dung and thus completed the task in a day.

Unfulfilled Promises, Dire Consequences

Augeas had promised Heracles a tenth of his herd if Heracles could clean the stable in one day. After Heracles had succeeded, Augeas refused to honor the agreement. When Heracles completed his labors, he killed Augeas and gave the kingdom to Augeas's son.

6. **Drive Out the Stymphalian Birds.** These maneating birds had taken over a forest in Arcadia. These birds had very long legs, steel-tipped feathers, and razor-sharp claws. They preyed on humans, shooting them with sharp feathers or attacking them with their beaks and claws. Heracles got rid of them by using a giant bronze rattle made by Hephaestus. The rattle's noise scared the birds and drove them from the forest. Because Hephaestus had helped him, though, Heracles didn't get credit for this feat.

7. **Capture the Cretan Bull.** The Cretan Bull was the beautiful bull given to Minos by Poseidon. After a long struggle, Heracles subdued the beast. Then he took it back to Tiryns and released it there.

8. **Capture the Mares of Diomedes.** Diomedes's mares were dangerous, maneating horses. Heracles succeeded in rounding up the mares. As he was driving them back to Tiryns, however, he was attacked by Diomedes. Heracles defeated Diomedes and fed him to his own horses. After they'd eaten their former owner, the horses became tame.

9. **Fetch Hippolyte's Girdle.** This girdle was a belt or sash owned by the queen of the Amazons, a fierce, warlike race of women. Heracles simply asked for the girdle, and Hippolyte gave it to him—an easy victory.

10. **Steal the Cattle of Geryon.** To complete this task, Heracles had to kill a two-headed watchdog and Eurytion the herdsman, a son of Ares who guarded the cattle. Then he had to engage in battle with Geryon, a monster with multiple heads and bodies; Heracles killed him with an arrow that had been dipped in the Lernaean Hydra's poisonous blood. Heracles encountered further obstacles as he drove the cattle back to Tiryns: The monster Cacus stole eight of the herd, and Hera sent a gadfly to scatter the cattle and a flood to swell a river they had to cross.

Another Death by Hera's Hands

Hera was furious that Heracles had obtained Hippolyte's girdle so easily. So she tricked the Amazons into thinking Heracles was stealing their queen. The Amazons rushed to attack him; Heracles, thinking the queen had betrayed him, killed her.

11. **Retrieve the Golden Apples of the Hesperides.** These apples belonged to Atlas's daughters, so Heracles convinced Atlas to

get the apples for him. While Atlas retrieved the apples, Heracles would hold the world on his own shoulders. Glad to be relieved of his heavy burden, Atlas agreed. When he returned with the apples, however, Atlas wasn't willing to take the world back upon his own shoulders. Heracles said he'd continue to bear the burden, but asked Atlas to take it back for just a moment so he could make himself more comfortable. Atlas did—and Heracles ran away with the apples.

12. **Fetch Cerberus from the Underworld.** Eurystheus charged Heracles with bringing the Underworld's three-headed guard dog back alive. With guidance from Athena, Hermes, and Hestia, Heracles entered the Underworld and crossed the river Styx. He asked Hades for permission to take Cerberus back to the world of the living. Hades agreed, but only if Heracles could overpower the monstrous dog without the use of weapons. (In some myths, Heracles must fight Hades before he can try to catch Cerberus.) Heracles wrestled Cerberus barehanded, subdued the creature, and carried it out of the Underworld. Eurystheus was terrified of the monster, however, and Heracles returned Cerberus to the Underworld.

After many years of laboring at near-impossible tasks, Heracles was finally purified of his family's murder. As the oracle had foretold, he'd also gained immortality. First, however, he had to live out the span of his mortal life. Before he became fully immortal, Heracles had several more adventures. He joined the Argonauts, killed several Giants, challenged Dionysus to a drinking contest (and lost), founded a city, and more.

CACUS VERSUS HERACLES

The most famous myth involving Cacus tells of his encounter with the hero Heracles. For one of his twelve labors, Heracles had to steal cattle from Geryon (another monster) and drive them back to Greece. Heracles successfully stole the cattle and was on his way home when he stopped to rest by a river. As the hero slept, Cacus spotted the magnificent herd and decided he wanted the cattle. He stole four bulls and four heifers. As Hermes had done in another myth, Cacus drove the cattle backward to mask their trail.

When Heracles awoke and saw that some of the cattle were missing, he searched for them, but Cacus's trick sent him in the wrong direction. Just when Heracles had almost given up, some of the cattle in his herd mooed, and a cow hidden in Cacus's cave answered their calls.

Realizing that his hiding place had been discovered, Cacus blocked the cave's entrance with a giant boulder. But that didn't stop Heracles; he broke off the mountaintop to expose the cave's interior. Cacus and Heracles fought; Cacus used fire and Heracles used boulders and tree branches. Cacus produced so much smoke that it was difficult for Heracles to see his target. He jumped into the cave where the smoke was thickest. He found Cacus there and strangled the monster to death.

HERACLES'S DEATH AND IMMORTALITY

Heracles's mortal life ended tragically. He married a woman named Deianeira, and while the couple was traveling, a Centaur named

Nessus tried to abduct her. Heracles shot Nessus with poisoned arrows. The dying Centaur gave Deianeira his blood-soaked shirt and told her that, if her husband wore it, he would become passionate for her. Later, Deianeira came to believe that Heracles was having an affair, and she gave him the shirt, hoping to rekindle his interest in her. As soon as the poison touched his skin, Heracles began writhing in pain as the flesh was ripped off his bones. He tore up trees to build his own funeral pyre and asked to be burned alive there. Heracles's mortal body burned, but his immortal body ascended to Mount Olympus.

Figure, from *Heracles Killing the Stymphalian Birds,* Albrecht Durer, ca. 1500

ANCIENT FEUDS: ATHENA VERSUS ARES

Bringing Sibling Rivalry to a Whole New Level

G

Ares was the god of war and his half sister Athena was the goddess of war. How could two deities enjoy dominion over the same realm? The answer lies in the different aspects of war that appealed to each. Ares loved the bloodshed and destruction that war brought. Although Athena was a skilled fighter, she preferred peace; she stood for justice and the ideals for which battles were fought. Athena enjoyed the intellectual side of war, the strategy and planning, whereas Ares preferred the chaos and physical exertion of an actual battle. Because of their different approaches to war, these two deities often found themselves in conflict.

One example of their animosity appears in accounts of the Trojan War. Ares joined the Trojan forces, while Athena fought with the Greeks. During a battle, Ares was fighting beside Hector (the best Trojan warrior) when he came face to face with Diomedes (not his son but the king of Aetolia). This Diomedes was held in high regard by the Greeks as a magnificent warrior.

Ares and Diomedes met in combat. Their fight caught Athena's attention. Athena used Hades's helmet of invisibility to intervene and set Ares's spear off course. This allowed Diomedes to strike, and his blow wounded Ares severely. The injury forced Ares to leave the battlefield and return to Mount Olympus, where Zeus healed him.

At another point in the war, Ares attacked Athena with his spear. But the spear hit Athena's protective, magical aegis. The spear didn't hurt Athena, but it did make her angry. She picked up a boulder and hurled it at Ares. Stunned by the blow, Ares collapsed. Aphrodite saw him fall and tried to help him escape. But Athena, still angry, attacked Aphrodite and struck her the old-fashioned way—using her bare fist.

A MURDER TRIAL

It probably comes as no surprise that Ares, in light of his hunger for blood and destruction, was once put on trial for the murder of Alirrothios, the son of Poseidon and Euryte, a nymph.

One day, Alirrothios came across Ares's daughter Alcippe near a spring. His lust for her culminated in rape. Ares was livid when he learned of this crime against his daughter. (According to some accounts, he witnessed the violation.) Ares killed Alirrothios to avenge Alcippe. Because Ares had killed his son, Poseidon took Ares to court for murder.

The trial was held on the hill overlooking the spot where the killing had occurred. The gods gathered in a tribunal and listened to both sides of the case. After deliberating, the tribunal acquitted Ares of murder.

The site of Ares's trial became known as the Areopagus, or "hill of Ares." The Areopagus was the meeting place of the council that governed Athens. During the era of Athenian democracy, the Areopagus was also the site of a court that tried cases of murder and other serious crimes. The court had approximately 250 members, and its decisions were final.

Another Version of Alirrothios's Death

Some myths tell an entirely different story regarding the death of Alirrothios. In these versions, a dispute began when Attica was allotted to Athena instead of Poseidon. Poseidon sent Alirrothios to cut down Athena's sacred olive trees. But the ax flew out of his hands and cut off his own head.

ARES IMPRISONED

Poseidon had two sons who were Giants, Otus and Ephialtes, known for wreaking havoc among the gods and goddesses. One of their exploits involved the capture and imprisonment of Ares. The story of Ares's imprisonment begins with the death of Adonis, a beautiful young man for whom Aphrodite felt great love. Some myths say her love was romantic and passionate; others say her love for the youth was that of a mother for her son. Regardless, Ares was unhappy with the attention his lover paid to Adonis. So while Adonis was hunting on Mount Lebanon, Ares transformed himself into a wild boar and gored Adonis to death.

Life and Death by a Boar

The manner of Adonis's death brought his life full circle; his birth was also caused by a boar. Adonis was a child of incest; his grandfather Theias was tricked into impregnating his own daughter, Myrrha. When Theias discovered what had happened, he tried to kill Myrrha. The gods protected her, however, by changing her into a tree. Adonis was born when a wild boar charged the tree, splitting it in two and allowing Adonis to emerge.

Some myths say that Otus and Ephialtes were upset by the death of Adonis because he'd been entrusted to their care by Aphrodite. Or perhaps they simply admired the beautiful youth, as most did. Whatever the reason, the two Giants set out to punish Ares for killing Adonis.

They captured Ares and bound him with chains. Then, they imprisoned him in a bronze cauldron (or jar) and left him there. Ares suffered in this prison for thirteen long months. The Giants' stepmother, Eriboea, eventually told Hermes where Ares was. The clever Hermes was able to slip past the two Giants and release Ares.

Immeasurable Strength

Otus and Ephialtes were so strong that nothing—not even the gods—could harm them. According to one version of this story, Artemis had to trick them into killing each other before Ares could be rescued.

Although his long imprisonment nearly caused Ares to lose his appetite for war, he soon recovered and returned to his bloodthirsty ways.

PERSEUS

Family Man, Monster-Slayer, Hero of Men

G

The poet Homer referred to Perseus as the "most renowned of all men"—and with good reason. Perseus was kind, faithful to his wife, and loyal to his mother and his family. He was also a fearsome slayer of monsters. Perseus was a model man and the epitome of a hero.

PROTECTING HIS MOTHER

Perseus was born to Danae and Zeus. When Danae was still a virgin, her father heard a prophecy that Danae's son would one day kill him, so he imprisoned his daughter in a tower to keep her away from men. But Zeus managed to get to her and their union produced Perseus. Danae's father locked Danae and her son in a chest and cast them out to sea, but they were saved by a kind fisherman.

Later, King Polydectes wanted a sexual relationship with Danae, but she wanted nothing to do with him. He was relentless in his pursuit, however, and Perseus defended his mother. Polydectes knew that he was no match for Perseus, so he devised a plan to get the young man out of the way. He pretended he was going to marry another woman and demanded lavish wedding gifts from his subjects. Perseus couldn't afford such a gift, but he offered to get the king anything he wanted. Polydectes told Perseus to bring him Medusa's head. This Gorgon was such a formidable monster that Polydectes was sure that Perseus's quest would kill him.

However, Perseus was favored by the gods; he had both Athena and Hermes on his side, and they helped him to overcome and kill Medusa. (See "Medusa: The Witch with a Bad Hair Day" to find out how Perseus accomplished his task.) When Perseus returned home, he found that Polydectes was still persecuting Danae, forcing her to work as a slave in his palace. Perseus showed Polydectes the head of Medusa and turned the king to stone.

RESCUING A DAMSEL IN DISTRESS

Perseus met his bride in the true fashion of a hero—he rescued her. Andromeda was a beautiful young woman, daughter of the king of Joppa. Her mother Cassiopeia was proud of her daughter's beauty, but she went too far and declared that her daughter was more beautiful than the Nereids. The offended sea nymphs complained to Poseidon, who sent Cetus, a sea monster, to attack the coast.

In great distress, the king consulted an oracle and learned that the only way to stop Cetus was to offer his daughter as a sacrifice to the monster. The king reluctantly complied and ordered that Andromeda be chained to the foot of a cliff by the sea. As Cetus approached Andromeda to devour her, Perseus flew in on winged sandals and used Hermes's sword to kill the monster.

Eternal Love

Andromeda and Perseus stayed together even after their deaths. Athena placed Andromeda in the sky as a constellation, along with Perseus, her parents, and Cetus.

Andromeda and Perseus were married and lived happily together. Unlike most husbands in mythology, Perseus was faithful to his wife for as long as he lived. Together they had a son, Perses.

A PROPHECY RETURNS

Perseus, a family man through and through, went to Argos to visit his grandfather, Acrisius. Even though his grandfather had tried to have him and his mother killed, Perseus had no hard feelings. Acrisius, on the other hand, hearing about his grandson's journey to Argos and remembering the prophecy that Danae's son would kill him, fled in fear.

Perseus followed Acrisius to Larissa, a city in Thessaly. Upon his arrival, he learned that the local king's father had died and funeral games were being held in his honor. Perseus joined in the funeral games, entering the discus-throwing competition. During the games, Perseus threw a discus that struck Acrisius, accidentally killing him. The old prophecy had been fulfilled.

With the death of Acrisius, Perseus gained the throne of Argos. He was so ashamed of the fact that he'd killed his own grandfather, however, that he wanted nothing to do with Argos. He traded kingdoms and became king of Tiryns instead.

THESEUS

An Athenian Legend and a True Hero

G

Theseus, the greatest Athenian hero, was the son of Aethra, a mortal woman. His father was either Aegeus (king of Athens) or Poseidon—or both. On the night of his conception, Aethra lay with both Aegeus and Poseidon—*on the same night*. Some myths hold that the son she bore had an immortal father and a mortal one.

Aethra lived in Troezen. When she was pregnant with Theseus, Aegeus showed her a great boulder. Beneath the boulder, he said, he had placed his sword and sandals. He told her that if her child was a boy, he could become heir to the Athenian throne if he could lift the boulder, remove the sword and sandals, and bring them to him. Then Aegeus returned to Athens.

When Theseus reached manhood, his mother showed him the boulder. He easily picked it up and retrieved the sword and sandals. Saying goodbye to his mother, he set out for Athens to meet his father for the first time.

THE JOURNEY TO ATHENS

Theseus could travel to Athens by sea or by land. The sea route was easier and safer, but—young hero that he was—Theseus chose the more dangerous land route. Along the way, he overcame many challenges from robbers, murderers, and monsters. In each case, Theseus delivered justice by turning the tables on those who attacked him.

At Epidaurus, Theseus encountered Periphetes, son of Hephaestus, who possessed a huge club that he used to attack and kill passersby. When Periphetes attacked him, Theseus managed to wrestle away the club and kill the bandit with his own weapon. Theseus kept the club, which became one of his emblematic weapons.

Theseus next came upon a vicious Giant named Sinis, who robbed and killed travelers. The Giant would bend down two pine trees, tie his victim between the two trees, and then let the trees spring upright, ripping the traveler in half. Theseus overcame the Giant and killed him by his own method. He also raped Sinis's daughter, Perigune, who later gave birth to Theseus's son Melanippus.

At Crommyon, Theseus was attacked by a huge, monstrous sow. Most mortals ran away in terror from this beast, but Theseus stood his ground and killed the sow with Aegeus's sword.

Next to block Theseus's way was Sciron, a robber who waited for travelers on a narrow path along a cliff's edge. He demanded that travelers wash his feet before he'd allow them to pass. When a traveler bent down before him, Sciron kicked the person over the cliff, where a sea monster (in some versions, a giant turtle) consumed the unfortunate traveler. Theseus, however, didn't fall for Sciron's trick. He pretended to comply, but as soon as he positioned himself in front of Sciron, Theseus took hold of Sciron's legs and threw the robber over the cliff.

Theseus's next assailant was Cercyon, king of Eleusis. This man challenged all passersby to a wrestling match, promising his kingdom to anyone who could beat him. His opponent always lost, however, and was always put to death. Theseus, a great wrestler, won the match, killing Cercyon and winning his kingdom.

Valuing Skill Over Strength

Cercyon had divine blood: According to different myths, he was the son of Poseidon or Hephaestus or the grandson of Apollo. He won his wrestling matches due to his incredible strength. Theseus, though not as strong, had better technique, so their contest illustrates the triumph of skill over brute strength.

Finally, Theseus happened upon an innkeeper named Procrustes. At first, the innkeeper seemed kind and hospitable, telling travelers that he had a marvelous bed that was a perfect fit for whoever slept in it. When a traveler lay down, however, Procrustes made that traveler fit the bed: A tall traveler would have his legs cut off, and a short traveler would be stretched or hammered like metal to fit. (Some myths say he had two beds, a long one and a short one, to ensure he could always murder his guests by this method.) Theseus turned the tables on Procrustes by making him fit his own bed (the myths don't say whether Procrustes was too tall or too short), killing him in the process.

RETURN TO THE THRONE

After a long and dangerous journey, Theseus finally reached Athens, but his trials were not over. Although he was welcomed warmly, he had not yet revealed himself to Aegeus. Aegeus was married to Medea, a skillful witch who wanted her own son to take over the throne. When Theseus arrived in Athens, Medea immediately recognized him as the rightful heir to the throne. She convinced her husband to distrust the newcomer.

Aegeus sent Theseus on a mission to kill the Cretan Bull, an exploit he believed would kill the young man. Always hungry for adventure, Theseus eagerly accepted the mission. Because he was such a skilled wrestler, Theseus overcame the bull by wrestling it to the ground. Then he tied a rope around its neck and led it back to Athens, where he presented the bull to Aegeus.

Of course, Medea was furious that the young man was still alive, so she decided to take matters into her own hands. At a banquet to celebrate Theseus's success, she poisoned the hero's cup. Just as Theseus was about to drink, Aegeus, who knew the cup was poisoned, recognized the sandals Theseus was wearing. The king dashed the cup from his son's hand.

Aegeus officially recognized Theseus as his son and named him as his successor. Medea was exiled (or fled) from Athens.

Pallas's Rebellion

Even though Aegeus chose Theseus as his successor, Aegeus's brother Pallas wanted the throne for himself. Pallas raised an army of supporters and rebelled. To stop the rebellion, Theseus had to kill several of his cousins and force his uncle out of Athens.

Theseus had many other adventures. He slew the Minotaur, abducted Helen, and was trapped in the Underworld with his friend Pirithous until he was rescued by Heracles. Some myths name him as one of the Argonauts. Theseus abducted and married Hippolyte, queen of the Amazons. (The abduction caused a war between the

Amazons and Athens.) Aphrodite caused his second wife, Phaedra, to fall in love with her stepson Hippolytus, who rejected her. Phaedra falsely told Theseus that Hippolytus had tried to rape her, and Theseus either killed his son directly or cursed him, causing a sea monster to frighten Hippolytus's horses, which bolted and dragged him to his death.

JASON

Leader of the Argonauts

G

Jason was the son of Aeson, who should have been the king of Iolcus. When Aeson's father died, however, Aeson's half brother Pelias usurped the throne. He spared Aeson but killed his sons. One son, Jason, was saved when his mother and her attendants encircled the new baby, crying and pretending that the child had been born dead. Jason was secretly sent to be raised by Chiron, a wise Centaur. Pelias still feared being overthrown, so he consulted an oracle, which warned him that a man with one sandal would cause his downfall.

When Jason grew up, he learned of his heritage and was determined to claim the throne. He left Chiron and journeyed to Iolcus. On the way, Jason had to cross a river. When he came to the river's edge, he met an old woman who asked him to carry her across. Jason agreed, but he lost a sandal in the process.

When Jason arrived in Iolcus, he wore his lone remaining sandal when he was presented to Pelias. Jason told the king that he had come to claim his birthright. Pelias could not kill Jason outright because of the laws of hospitality; plus he did not want to start a riot among Aeson's supporters. Therefore, Pelias replied that Jason could have the throne if he brought back the Golden Fleece of Chrysomallos, a magnificent winged ram. Jason agreed, and thus began the famous quest for the Golden Fleece.

Sneaky Hera

The old woman whom Jason carried across the river was actually Hera in disguise. Hera hated Pelias because he had never given her due reverence. Therefore, Hera supported Jason in his quest to regain the throne.

THE QUEST FOR THE GOLDEN FLEECE

Jason gathered some of the noblest and greatest heroes of Greece, including Heracles, to join him on his quest. Under the direction of Athena, they had a great ship built and named it the *Argo*. The band of heroes called themselves the Argonauts, or "sailors of the *Argo*." They set sail for Colchis, where the fleece was located, but the journey was long and fraught with many obstacles. The Argonauts dallied with the women of the island of Lemnos (Jason fathered twins there), got lost, fought battles, rescued the prophet Phineus from some Harpies, and got through the Symplegades (cliffs that crashed together, crushing any ships that attempted to sail between them).

Finally, the Argonauts landed in Colchis, where Jason claimed the fleece. Aeëtes, King of Colchis, told Jason he could have the fleece if he accomplished three tasks:

1. Yoke a team of fire-breathing oxen and use them to plow a field.
2. Plant a dragon's tooth in the plowed field.
3. Conquer the never-sleeping dragon that guarded the fleece.

Jason was favored by both Hera and Athena, who helped him on his quest. Athena summoned Eros to make Medea, a witch who was Aeëtes's daughter, fall madly in love with Jason. Medea became infatuated with the hero and helped him in each task:

- She gave him an ointment to protect his skin from the fire-breathing oxen.
- She warned Jason that the dragon's teeth, once planted, would create an army of warriors and told him how to defeat them. Jason threw a rock into the crowd of warriors. Confused, they attacked and killed each other.
- She gave Jason a sleeping potion that put the guardian dragon to sleep, and he was able to grab the fleece.

As soon as Jason had the fleece, the Argonauts left Colchis, taking Medea with them.

Aeëtes sent his son Apsyrtus and a fleet of ships to pursue the fleeing Argonauts. Again, Medea acted to help her lover. She sent word to her brother that she had been kidnapped and told him that he must rescue her at a particular location. When Apsyrtus went there to rescue his sister, Jason ambushed and killed him. At the same time, the Argonauts attacked and killed Apsyrtus's crew.

Macabre Myths

In another, more gruesome myth, Apsyrtus was just a boy while Jason was in Colchis. To aid the Argonauts' escape, Medea kidnapped her brother, chopped him into small pieces, and threw his remains in the water as they sailed away. Aeëtes had to collect all the pieces of his son for a proper burial—and he needed his ships to retrieve the pieces of his son's body—so the pursuit of the Argonauts was called off.

The Argonauts faced more challenges on the way home. They had to navigate between the whirlpool Charybdis and the cave-dwelling monster Scylla, face terrible sea storms, find their way back to the Mediterranean after being blown far off course, and defeat a terrible bronze Giant. But they eventually made it home to Iolcus.

HORRIFYING TRAGEDIES AND AN UNSUCCESSFUL HERO

While the Argonauts were on their quest, a rumor spread in Iolcus that their ship had sunk. Thinking that Jason was dead, Pelias killed Jason's younger brother and his father Aeson. This upset Jason's mother so much that she killed herself.

Faced with the deaths of his parents and brother, Jason knew that Pelias would never give up the throne. He agreed to let Medea get rid of him. Medea convinced Pelias's daughters that they could restore their father's youth and demonstrated what they needed to do: She killed a ram, cut it into pieces, and boiled those pieces. A little while later, a lamb leaped from the pot. Pelias's daughters did the same thing to their father. They cut him into pieces and boiled the pieces. But no young boy emerged from the pot; Pelias had been killed by his own family.

Even with Pelias out of the way, Jason did not get the throne. He and Medea were exiled from Iolcus due to the ghastly way in which they had disposed of Pelias. They fled to Corinth. There, Jason fell in love with Glauce, daughter of the king of Corinth, and planned to leave Medea to marry her. Medea gave Jason's new bride-to-be a poisoned dress and crown; when Glauce put them on, she was killed, along with her father, who rushed to save her. Medea then murdered the two children she'd had with Jason and escaped to Athens, leaving Jason to mourn his losses.

Because Jason had abandoned his wife, he lost Hera's favor. Although he did regain the throne of Iolcus for his son Thessalus, the rest of his life was unhappy. Eventually, Jason died when a timber from the *Argo* fell on him.

ODYSSEUS

King of Ithaca, Hero of the *Odyssey*

G

Odysseus was king of the island of Ithaca. Renowned for his cleverness, he fought on the Greek side during the Trojan War and came up with the ruse of the Trojan horse. The Homeric epic the *Odyssey* tells the story of Odysseus's long voyage home after the ten-year Trojan War. Trying to return to his faithful wife and son, Odysseus faced ten years of obstacles and adventures. His journey was so long and arduous because he had offended Poseidon—not a good idea if you're going to travel by sea.

During the first part of Odysseus's journey home, his men battled the Cicones. Although they won the fight, they sustained some casualties, losing six men from each ship. At another stop, Odysseus sent three men to scout the location. The scouting party encountered the lotus-eaters and joined them in a feast. The lotus put the men in a dream state that made them stop caring about going home; all they wanted was to eat more of the lotus. Odysseus had the men dragged back to the ships and tied down so they wouldn't jump overboard and swim back to the lotus-eaters' land.

FACING THE CYCLOPS POLYPHEMUS

Things took a serious turn for the worse when Odysseus's ships landed on an island inhabited by the Cyclopes—one-eyed, maneating Giants. The Cyclops Polyphemus was Poseidon's son. When

Odysseus and twelve of his men explored the island, they found a cave with a large amount of food stored in the back. Odysseus and his men settled in to wait for the cave's owner to return to ask him to share his food. But the cave's owner was Polyphemus.

Around dusk, Polyphemus returned with his flock of sheep. As was his routine, he drove the flock into the cave and blocked the entrance with a massive boulder. Odysseus asked the Cyclops for the hospitality due to him by the laws of the gods. Polyphemus answered Odysseus's request by seizing two of his men and devouring them.

The men could not kill Polyphemus because he was the only one strong enough to move the boulder away from the cave's entrance. In the morning, Polyphemus ate two more of Odysseus's men and then drove his flock outside. He then replaced the boulder, keeping the men trapped inside the cave, waiting their turn to become a meal for the Cyclops. But clever Odysseus devised a plan.

When Polyphemus returned with his flock that night, he ate two more men. Odysseus gave the Cyclops some strong wine the hero had with him. Polyphemus got drunk and asked Odysseus his name, to which Odysseus replied, "No-one." Polyphemus was grateful for the wine and promised to eat No-one last as his reward. Then he passed out. As the monster lay sleeping, Odysseus drove a stake through his single eye, blinding him. Polyphemus cried out that he was being murdered, and the other Cyclopes came running. When they asked who was attacking him, he answered, "No-one!" This answer made no sense, and the other Cyclopes left him alone.

In the morning, Polyphemus needed to let his flock out to graze, but he worried that the men would take advantage of his blindness and escape. So, after he'd moved the boulder, he blocked the entrance with his own body. As his sheep filed out one by one, he felt their backs to make sure that only the sheep were leaving. Because he couldn't see, however, he didn't notice that Odysseus and his six surviving men had tied themselves under the sheep's bellies. In this way, they escaped from the Cyclops's cave. They drove the sheep to their ship, loaded them on board, and set sail from the island.

As they sailed away, Polyphemus threw huge boulders at their ship, but because of his blindness he missed. Odysseus couldn't resist telling the Cyclops the real name of the hero who'd tricked him, shouting that it was the great Odysseus. In a rage, Polyphemus asked his father, Poseidon, to prevent Odysseus from ever getting home—or, if that wasn't possible, that all his men would be killed and his fleet destroyed. Poseidon took his son's prayers to heart and bedeviled Odysseus for the rest of his journey.

WINDY AEOLUS

Odysseus and his men visited Aeolus, a mortal to whom the gods had granted control of the winds, on his floating island, Aeolia. They stayed there for several days, and Odysseus entertained Aeolus with stories of his adventures. As a parting gift, Aeolus gave Odysseus a bag that held all of the winds except for the wind that blew toward Ithaca. As long as the other winds remained in the bag, Odysseus's ships would head straight home.

Odysseus guarded the bag day and night. When his fleet was almost at Ithaca, his men began to wonder what was in the bag. Since Odysseus kept such close watch on it, they reasoned it probably held a treasure. As Odysseus slept, the crew opened the bag, releasing all the winds it held. A violent storm blew them back to Aeolia. This time, Aeolus could not offer any help because he did not want to offend the god who opposed Odysseus.

TRICKY GIANTS

Odysseus arrived at the land of the Laestrygonians: savage, maneating Giants. At first, the locals seemed friendly; a young girl even gave the men directions to her parents' house. When the men arrived, they were met by a Giantess, who called for her husband. As soon as he arrived, he snatched one of the men and ate him.

The other men escaped and rushed back to their ships, with the Laestrygonians in hot pursuit. Before the fleet could sail away, the Giants hurled huge boulders at the ships, causing them to sink. They speared the men like fish and ate them. The only ship that got away was Odysseus's, which had been at a distance from the others.

TURNING MEN INTO SWINE

With just one ship remaining, Odysseus was wary of the other dangers he might encounter. The next time he landed on an island, the men drew lots to determine who would explore the island. Odysseus stayed on the ship.

The explorers came upon the witch Circe, who invited them to dine with her; she turned all the men into swine. One man escaped and told Odysseus what had happened. Determined to save his men, Odysseus went ashore alone. Hermes intercepted him and gave him a magic herb to protect him from Circe's magic. When her magic failed, Odysseus threatened to kill her for what she'd done. She begged him for mercy and offered to sleep with him. But Hermes had warned Odysseus that she would try to steal his manhood in bed, so the hero made her swear by the gods that she would not harm either him or his crew. He also demanded that she return his crew to their true form. She did as she was told and, surprisingly, became a gracious and hospitable hostess. Odysseus and his men stayed with her for an entire year.

Mistaken Identities and an Accidental Death

During his year on Circe's island, Odysseus had an affair with the witch. According to one myth, their son, Telegonus, eventually caused his father's death. As a young man, Telegonus went in search of his father. Mistaking Ithaca for a different island, he attacked it. When Odysseus defended his kingdom, Telegonus killed him.

ODYSSEUS'S OBSTACLE COURSE

Poseidon was determined to do whatever he could to prevent Odysseus from getting home. Before Odysseus returned to Ithaca, he encountered many other obstacles, adventures, and trials, including:

A Journey to the Underworld

Odysseus decided to speak with the shade of the prophet Tiresias to find out how to avoid other dangers on his trip home. Tiresias told him how to get safely past the cattle of Helios, Scylla, and Charybdis. He also told Odysseus how to make peace with Poseidon after he'd made it back to Ithaca. While he was in the Underworld, Odysseus also spoke with the shades of his mother, Agamemnon, and Achilles.

The Sirens

These female creatures sang beautiful, alluring songs as ships sailed past. When sailors steered closer, their ships were dashed against hidden rocks. On Circe's advice, Odysseus had his men plug their ears with wax so they wouldn't be tempted by the Sirens' singing. Odysseus wanted to hear the beautiful songs, so he had his men tie him to the ship's mast. When he heard the Sirens singing, he struggled to break free so he could go to them, but his bonds prevented him, keeping him and his ship safe.

After his ship passed them by and not a single sailor succumbed to their music, the Sirens became distraught. Thinking their spell had lost its power, they threw themselves into the sea and were never heard from again.

Scylla and Charybdis

Scylla was a maneating monster that lived in a cave in some sea cliffs, and Charybdis was a dangerous whirlpool. Sailors trying to pass them were usually caught by one or the other. When Odysseus's ship arrived at these dangers, he judged Scylla to be the lesser of the two evils and steered his ship closer to her side. Unfortunately, he got too close, and Scylla seized and devoured six of his crew.

The Cattle of Helios

Odysseus had been warned by both Circe and Tiresias not to touch the cattle on a certain island because they were sacred to Helios. When they approached this island, Odysseus told his men that they would not stop there, but the men threatened to mutiny and Odysseus was forced to give in. While they were ashore, the winds changed, and they couldn't leave. After a while, they ran out of food. Odysseus warned the men not to touch the sun god's cattle, but his crew figured it would be better to feast on the cattle and be killed by the gods than to die of starvation. Helios was furious and complained to Zeus, threatening to hide the sun in the Underworld if he wasn't avenged. When Odysseus's men set out to sea again, Zeus sent a storm that killed the entire crew. Odysseus's ship was pulled into Charybdis, and the hero barely escaped.

Calypso's Island

After Odysseus's ship was destroyed, he clung to a piece of wood and drifted for nine days. He landed on an island inhabited by the nymph Calypso. Calypso fell in love with Odysseus and kept him with her for seven years, promising him immortality if he stayed. But Odysseus yearned for home. Eventually, at Athena's request, Zeus sent Hermes to order Calypso to release Odysseus.

Return to Ithaca

Odysseus left Calypso's island on a raft and was nearly killed when Poseidon sent a storm. He washed up on the island of Scheria, where he was hospitably received by the Phaeacians, who eventually gave him passage home on one of their ships. When Odysseus finally reached Ithaca, he had to fight the suitors who had been living in his palace and trying to win the hand of his faithful wife Penelope (and with it his throne). He won the battle, with Athena's aid, and reclaimed both his wife and his kingdom.

Quick-Witted Penelope

Penelope was a clever woman, loyal to her husband throughout his twenty-year absence. When suitors pressed her to choose a new husband, she replied that she was weaving a burial shroud for her ailing father-in-law and would choose one of them after she had finished. Each day she wove, and each night she undid that day's weaving, forestalling the suitors until Odysseus could finally return.

ACHILLES, AGAMEMNON, AND OTHER IMPORTANT HEROES

Get to Know the Men the Ancients Idolized

G

Classical mythology tells of the exploits and adventures of many heroes. Here are some other heroes you're likely to meet in the myths.

ACHILLES

Achilles was the greatest hero on the Greek side of the Trojan War. He was the son of Peleus, king of the Myrmidons, and Thetis, a sea nymph. Zeus and Poseidon had both wooed Thetis, until Prometheus warned them that Thetis would give birth to a son who would become far greater than his father. Hearing that prophecy, the gods decided to leave Thetis alone.

When Achilles was born, his mother tried to make him immortal. According to one myth, she rubbed the baby with ambrosia and placed him on a fire to burn away his mortality, but she was interrupted by her husband before she was finished. The more famous story is that she dipped her son into the river Styx, holding him by one foot. The water made the boy impervious to harm—everywhere except for the heel that his mother grasped as she lowered him into the water. This is where the phrase *Achilles heel*—a small but serious weakness—comes from.

Achilles was raised by Chiron the Centaur, who'd also brought up Jason. He is a central figure of Homer's epic poem the *Iliad* (turn to "Heroes of the Trojan War" and "Ares" to read more of Achilles's story).

AGAMEMNON

He sacrificed his daughter Iphigenia to bring the winds that would allow his fleet to sail to Troy. During the Trojan War, Agamemnon commanded the Greek forces. After he returned home, he was murdered in his bath by his wife Clytemnestra and her lover Aegisthus.

MELEAGER

The hero who killed the Calydonian Boar, Meleager was also listed among the Argonauts.

NARCISSUS

A devastatingly handsome man, Narcissus scorned all who loved him. As punishment, the gods caused him to fall in love with his own reflection in a pool of water. When he realized that the object of his desire was a mere reflection and could not love him back, Narcissus committed suicide.

Catharsis with Tragedies

The Greek philosopher Aristotle believed that audiences enjoy tragedy because it causes them to feel pity and fear for the characters; by feeling these emotions through a story, they experience catharsis, a release of emotional tension. Examples of tragedy include the stories of Oedipus and Antigone.

OEDIPUS

Before Oedipus's birth, his parents, Laius and Jocasta, king and queen of Thebes, learned through an oracle that their son would kill his father and marry his mother. At the child's birth, Laius ordered a servant to abandon the child on a hillside to die, but the servant gave the helpless baby to a shepherd instead. When Oedipus came of age, he heard the same prophecy. Trying to avoid his fate, he left the city where he'd grown up and the people he believed were his parents, traveling toward Thebes. At a crossroads, he fought with a stranger and killed him; the man was Laius, his biological father. After Oedipus solved the riddle of the Sphinx, he became king of Thebes and married the recently widowed queen Jocasta, his biological mother. When Oedipus learned that he'd actually fulfilled the prophecy he'd tried to avoid, he blinded himself.

ORESTES

Son of Agamemnon, Orestes avenged his father's death by murdering his own mother, Clytemnestra. He was pursued by the Erinyes for his crime until Athena cast a tie-breaking vote in Orestes's favor at his trial.

ORPHEUS

A master musician, Orpheus ventured into the Underworld to rescue his wife, Eurydice, who'd been killed by a poisonous snake. (Turn to "Escaping Death: Mortals Who Traveled to the Underworld" to read about how that worked out.)

PELOPS

When Pelops was a child, his father, Tantalus, cut him to pieces and made a stew of his flesh, offering it to the gods as a feast. The gods weren't fooled and restored the boy to life. Only Demeter, distracted by the absence of Persephone, took a bite of meat; this missing piece of Pelops's shoulder was replaced by a piece of ivory. The gods taught Pelops how to drive a chariot, and he won his wife in a chariot race (although he cheated by having the linchpins removed from his opponent's chariot to make the wheels fall off). A great warrior, Pelops conquered the area known as the Peloponnese. Later, the Greeks carried his bones to Troy because of a prophecy that they would win the war if they did so.

THE ORIGINS OF THE TROJAN WAR

The Famous Ancient Conflict Explained

G

The Trojan War—a ten-year conflict between the Achaeans (a collective name for the various Greek forces) and the Trojans—was one of the most famous events in classical mythology. It was a long, bloody, and destructive war that caused numerous tragedies. Yet it was also an occasion for warriors to prove their heroism and for the gods to help their favorites.

Several seemingly unrelated events fit together like a jigsaw puzzle and caused the Trojan War. It all began at the wedding of Peleus and Thetis—parents of the Greek hero Achilles.

A FAILED MARRIAGE

The wedding of Peleus, a mortal king, and Thetis, a sea goddess, was a grand affair. Nearly all the gods and goddesses attended, as did many mortals.

Eris, the goddess of strife and discord, was not invited to the wedding. In fact, Zeus instructed Hermes to stop Eris at the door if she appeared. When Eris was prevented from entering, she threw a golden apple inscribed with the words "for the fairest" into the crowd. Athena, Aphrodite, and Hera each considered herself to be the fairest and therefore the apple's rightful owner. A dispute broke out among the goddesses. None of the other deities wanted to get involved; if they chose one goddess, the other two would be angry and out for revenge. So Zeus ordered Hermes to lead them to the handsome young prince Paris, and he would settle the dispute. Paris chose Aphrodite because she promised him the most beautiful woman in the world—who happened to be Helen of Troy.

HELEN OF TROY

Helen, the daughter of Zeus and Leda, always had numerous suitors, and her stepfather, King Tyndareus of Sparta, worried that this competition would start a war among the princes of Greece. So Tyndareus, advised by the clever Odysseus, made all of Helen's suitors swear that they would support and defend whoever became her husband. The suitors drew straws, and the winner was Menelaus. He married Helen and, after the death of Tyndareus, became king of Sparta.

PARIS WANTS HIS PRIZE

Even though Helen was already married, Paris was determined to collect the prize promised to him by Aphrodite. Against everyone's advice, Paris traveled to Sparta. When he arrived, he was welcomed warmly by Menelaus.

While Paris was visiting, Menelaus had to leave Sparta to attend a funeral. He left Helen behind, never imagining she could be in danger. Paris saw his chance. He grabbed Helen and fled Sparta. (Some myths say he also stole treasure from the palace.)

Menelaus and Odysseus traveled to Troy to demand Helen's return. King Priam did not want war with the Greeks, but his fifty sons appealed to him to protect Paris's right to Helen, who had been promised to him by Aphrodite herself. Outvoted, Priam refused to return Helen and the stolen treasure.

HEADED FOR TROY

When Menelaus returned to Sparta, he immediately called upon Helen's former suitors who had sworn to support him. Though wary of the situation, they agreed to abide by the oath. An army of Greek forces was assembled, and Menelaus named his brother Agamemnon commander in chief.

Protesilaus's Story

The first Greek to step ashore at Troy was a warrior named Protesilaus. A prophecy had stated that the first Greek to set foot on Trojan soil would be the first Greek to die there. Later, the Trojan warrior Hector killed Protesilaus, making him the first Greek casualty of the war.

Menelaus rounded up more than a thousand ships to sail for Troy. The winds were not in their favor, however, and the ships could not leave the harbor. As you read in "Artemis," Agamemnon had previously offended Artemis. A seer told Agamemnon that he must sacrifice his daughter Iphigenia to appease Artemis and gain favorable winds. Agamemnon complied, an act that would cause trouble for him later.

The Greek fleet arrived at Troy. Deciding that the best tactic would be to cut off the supply of provisions to the city, the Greeks attacked the surrounding towns. These battles took place over the course of nine years. It was only during the war's tenth year that the Greeks attacked Troy directly.

ENTER THE OLYMPIANS

The gods and goddesses took an intense interest in the Trojan War. Many of them chose sides and helped their favorites when they could. The gods were split in their choices, though, which is one reason the war dragged on for so long.

Many of the Olympians supported the Greeks. Poseidon sided with the Greeks because he still held an old grudge against Troy; he never forgot that an earlier king had refused to pay him for helping to build the city's protective walls. Hera and Athena also had a grudge against Troy; Paris had given the golden apple to Aphrodite and not to one of them. Hermes and Hephaestus also supported the Greeks.

The Weaknesses of the Gods

Even the gods and goddesses weren't invincible during wartime. At least two deities were wounded on the battlefield. Ares was struck by Diomedes's spear, and Aphrodite was hit either by Athena or by Diomedes as she tried to help Ares leave the battlefield.

The Trojans also had the support of several gods. Aphrodite, winner of the golden apple, stuck with Paris and sided with the Trojans. Apollo and Artemis also favored the Trojans. Ares had no particular allegiance but was most often seen fighting with the Trojans, probably because his lover Aphrodite supported them.

Other Olympians—including Hades, Hestia, Demeter, and Zeus—remained neutral.

HEROES OF THE TROJAN WAR

The Bravest of Ancient Men

G

The Trojan War brought together some of the most famous heroes of classical mythology. There were legendary fighters on both sides:

- **Hector**. The oldest son of King Priam, Hector was the best warrior on the Trojan side. A brave, noble man, he had been in favor of returning Helen to her husband. But when war became inevitable, Hector was a vigorous and formidable defender of his city. He killed Protesilaus, the first Greek to die in the war. He also killed Achilles's best friend, Patroclus, an act that led to his own downfall. Hector was favored and protected by Apollo, but even Apollo couldn't protect him from Achilles.

- **Achilles**. He was the greatest warrior among the Greeks during this war. Achilles killed a great number of enemies, but when he came into conflict with Agamemnon over a concubine, he got angry and refused to fight. When Achilles heard of his friend Patroclus's death, he swore an oath to kill Hector. He rejoined the war with a fury that drove him to kill countless Trojans, including Hector. Achilles defiled Hector's body. For days, he dragged Hector's corpse behind his chariot as he drove around and around the walls of Troy. Later, Achilles was killed by an arrow shot by Paris, which hit him in the one spot where he was vulnerable: his heel. Some myths say that Apollo guided the arrow to the fatal spot.

The Gods Hit Pause

After more than a week of watching Achilles abuse Hector's dead body, the gods had had enough. They sent Iris, a messenger goddess, and Thetis, Achilles's mother, to order Achilles to let King Priam ransom his son's body. Achilles complied, and the war paused for twelve days so that Hector could be given proper funeral rites.

- **Patroclus.** Achilles's best friend, he had been raised in the wilderness with Achilles by the Centaur Chiron. During the Trojan War, he was a warrior on the Greek side. When Achilles refused to fight, Patroclus wore Achilles's armor and took his place in battle. Patroclus fought well, but he was eventually killed by Hector.
- **Aeneas.** A son of Aphrodite, he was second only to Hector on the Trojan side. A valiant warrior with many successes on the battlefield, Aeneas fought to the bitter end, even as Troy burned around him. He was one of the few Trojans to survive the war, and he led the other survivors to their new home.
- **Diomedes.** Besides Achilles, he was the best warrior on the Greek side. One of Helen's former suitors, he was bound by his oath to fight with the Greeks. Diomedes killed the Trojan prince Pandarus, wounded Aeneas, and wounded both Ares and Aphrodite—in just one day on the field.
- **Agamemnon.** He was commander in chief of the Greek forces. He killed Antiphus, one of Priam's sons. Although Agamemnon was an authoritative leader, he came into conflict with Achilles during the war's last year over a woman, Briseis, whom Achilles felt he'd won as a war prize.

- **Odysseus**. A skilled tactician and diplomat, he often soothed tempers when different Greek factions fell into conflict. Along with Ajax, Odysseus retrieved the slain Achilles's body and armor from the middle of a fierce battle. He was favored by Athena, who often helped him.
- **Ajax of Salamis**. Often referred to as Ajax the Great, this Greek warrior twice fought Hector. Zeus declared the first battle a draw; in the second battle, Hector disarmed Ajax, who had to withdraw from the fighting. After Ajax and Odysseus retrieved Achilles's body, Odysseus was awarded Achilles's armor. Athena struck the furious Ajax mad, and he slaughtered a herd of sheep, believing that they were the Greeks who had denied him the honor of Achilles's armor. When he regained his senses and realized what he'd done, he committed suicide.
- **Ajax of Locris**. Also known as Ajax the Lesser, he defiled a temple of Athena after Troy fell. The Trojan princess Cassandra had sought sanctuary in the temple and was clinging to a statue of the goddess. Ajax dragged her from the temple (in some versions, he raped her first). He was killed by Athena on his journey home from Troy.
- **Nestor**. On the Greek side, Nestor was an older man known for his wise advice. Although too old to engage in actual combat, he led his troops in a chariot and carried a golden shield. Nestor's son Antilochus, who had been one of Helen's suitors, was killed in the war.
- **Teucer**. Although he was King Priam's nephew, he fought with his half brother Ajax of Salamis on the Greek side of the war. He was known as a skilled archer, yet every time he shot an arrow at Hector, Apollo deflected it.

THE FALL OF TROY

No Great Empire Lasts Forever

G

For nine long years, the Greeks succeeded in conquering the towns around Troy, but they hadn't conquered the city itself. The siege dragged on. So much blood had already been spilled; men missed their families; and exhaustion was taking its toll. Something had to give. The tenth year was the turning point of the war. Just as several factors combined to cause the war, a number of different events worked together to bring the war to its close.

TROJANS AHEAD

Hector's death was a severe blow to the Trojans. Soon after, however, the Greeks lost Achilles (killed by Paris with Apollo's help) and Ajax of Salamis, who killed himself. Also, Amazon warriors arrived to help the Trojan cause. These events did not bode well for the Greeks. However, they were far from giving up. If anything, they became even more motivated.

AN INSIDER'S SECRETS

Led by Odysseus, the Greeks captured Helenus, Priam's son and one of Troy's chief prophets. Helenus revealed that the Greek forces would never defeat Troy without the help of Achilles's son

Neoptolemus, and Philoctetes, who owned the bow and arrows of Heracles. Helenus also told the Greeks that Troy could not fall as long as the Palladium stood within the city.

Odysseus and Diomedes volunteered to fetch Neoptolemus and Philoctetes. First they went to Scyrus to recruit the young Neoptolemus. This was an easy task, for the young man was eager to join the army and live up to his father's honorable name. Next they traveled to the island of Lemnos to get Philoctetes, who proved to be more difficult to recruit. Philoctetes was bitter toward the Greeks, especially Odysseus, for abandoning him on the island years before. But the ghost of Heracles visited Philoctetes and told him it was his duty to help the Greeks, so he agreed to join the Greek cause.

What Was the Palladium?

The Palladium was a sacred statue erected by Athena to honor her young friend Pallas, whom Athena had inadvertently killed. Originally the Palladium was placed in the heavens, but later it fell to Earth and landed on the site of the future city of Troy. The statue was believed to protect the city from destruction.

When the group returned to Troy, Odysseus and Diomedes devised a scheme to steal the Palladium from inside the city walls. They disguised themselves, and under cover of night, snuck into Troy and removed the statue unchallenged.

Although the Greeks accomplished the tasks outlined by Helenus, Troy did not fall. They still needed a plan.

THE FALL OF TROY

Odysseus came up with a plan to get the Greeks into Troy. Under Athena's direction, the Greeks built a gigantic wooden horse with a hollow body. Odysseus and an elite group of Greek warriors hid inside the horse. Their Greek companions took the horse to the city gates and left it there with an inscription explaining it was dedicated to Athena.

The Greek army then withdrew from sight, pretending to sail away. The Trojans weren't quite sure what to do with the horse. Some wanted to destroy it. Others wanted to bring it inside, and still others could hardly contain their curiosity.

A raggedly dressed Greek soldier appeared. He said his name was Sinon and that the Greek army had planned to sacrifice him to Athena, but he had escaped. Athena was furious with the Greeks, he explained, because they had stolen the Palladium. As if disclosing a great secret, Sinon told the Trojans that the Greeks had built the great wooden horse as an offering to Athena, but that they'd purposely built it to be too big to fit through the city's gates. The horse would replace the Palladium and bring the Trojans victory.

Most of the Trojans agreed that they should try to get the horse inside the city walls. One man, however, spoke out against the idea. The prophet Laocoon, wary of what the horse would bring, warned the Trojans not to trust the Greeks. To emphasize his point, Laocoon threw his spear at the horse. Just then a huge monster rose up from the sea and devoured Laocoon and his sons.

To the Trojans, Laocoon's death appeared to be a direct result of his attack on the horse. They reasoned that the horse must indeed be an offering to Athena; when Laocoon attacked the horse, she was offended and sent the sea monster to punish him. Athena did send the sea monster to kill Laocoon, but not because he had desecrated her monument—she just wanted to shut him up.

Helen's Wisdom

Some myths say that Helen suspected the Greeks' trick. At night, she ventured out to inspect the horse and mimicked the voices of some of the Greek warriors' wives, trying to get the men to respond. Odysseus was able to keep his men quiet, and they were not discovered.

The Trojans decided to bring the horse into the city. When the horse was inside Troy's walls, they celebrated what they believed was their sure victory. No one noticed Sinon release the Greek warriors who were hidden inside the horse.

Outside Troy, the Greek army, which had only pretended to sail away, quickly reassembled. The warriors who'd hidden in the horse opened the city gates—and in rushed the Greeks. They sacked Troy, destroying the city completely and killing or capturing all the Trojans they could find. Priam tried to take refuge at the altar of Zeus, but he was brutally murdered by Neoptolemus, Achilles's son. Hector's infant son Astyanax was thrown from Troy's high walls. Trojan women—including Hecuba (the queen), Andromache (Hector's wife), and Cassandra (a Trojan princess)—were enslaved. Some myths say that Ajax of Locris raped Cassandra on the altar of Athena.

ANGERING THE GODS

After they'd helped the Greeks defeat Troy, several of the Olympians were appalled at the warriors' sacrilegious behavior. The gods and goddesses who'd once supported the Greeks decided to punish them. Even though the Greeks had won the war, they didn't fare much better than the Trojans. After ten years of fighting, not many Greek soldiers made it home alive.

Poseidon called up a great storm, which destroyed much of the Greek fleet. Some of the remaining ships were wrecked on the rocky shores of Euboea, where they had been guided by a false beacon. Other ships, blown far off course by the storm, were lost for years. Some Greeks did make it home—and later wished they hadn't:

- Diomedes returned home to Argos to find that his wife had taken another man as her lover. He was exiled from his own country.
- Teucer arrived home safely but was not allowed to land. His father forbade him to enter the country because of his deeds during the war.
- In order to arrive home safely, Idomeneus promised Poseidon he would sacrifice the first living creature he encountered after reaching his homeland. Poseidon allowed him safe passage, but when the ship landed, the first to meet Idomeneus was his son, happy and excited that his father was home. Bound by his promise, Idomeneus sacrificed his son to Poseidon. For this act, Idomeneus was banished from his homeland.
- Agamemnon returned home to find that his wife, Clytemnestra, had taken a lover. Clytemnestra, still furious over the sacrifice of her daughter Iphigenia, murdered Agamemnon in his bath.

- It took Odysseus ten years to get home to Ithaca. Although Odysseus was supported by Athena, he was opposed by Poseidon—and his journey home was fraught with dangers.

Nestor's Journey

Nestor, who disapproved of the Greeks' conduct during the sacking of Troy, made it home safely and in good time. Later, Odysseus's son Telemachus visits Nestor seeking information about his father.

The Trojan War was a long, bloody, and vicious conflict that destroyed a city and wasted many lives. It was the occasion for great acts of heroism and horrifying acts of brutality. The losses were catastrophic, and victory meant very little. In some ways, the fall of Troy signaled the end of the world the Greeks had known, because the city's destruction eventually led to the founding of Rome.

COMPARING GREEK AND ROMAN MYTHOLOGIES

Shared Stories and New Tales

G R

Early in Rome's history, the ancient Romans had a religion that was completely their own. As time passed, however, extensive changes occurred within this religion. As Romans conquered neighboring territories, they absorbed some aspects of local religions, and as Greek literature became known in Rome, it influenced Roman religion. Greek mythology was assimilated into Roman mythology to fill in gaps in the latter; eventually, Romans adopted (and adapted) Greek myths on a broad scale.

Similarities and Differences

While many of the stories are essentially the same in Greek and Roman mythologies, the names are different. However, the Romans also had their own myths, separate from those of the Greeks.

Although the Romans borrowed heavily from Greek mythology, they kept their own names for the gods and goddesses. To gain a very basic knowledge of Roman mythology, just examine the Roman and Greek counterparts in the following table. Because Roman myths are so similar to Greek ones, knowing the Roman equivalents of Greek names gives you a head start in understanding Roman mythology.

GREEK NAME	ROMAN NAME
Aphrodite	Venus
Hera	Juno
Apollo	Sol
Heracles	Hercules
Ares	Mars
Hermes	Mercury
Artemis	Diana
Hestia	Vesta
Athena	Minerva
Muses	Camenae
Cronus	Saturn
Odysseus	Ulysses
Demeter	Ceres
Pan	Faunus
Dionysus	Bacchus
Parcae (Fates)	Moirai
Eos	Aurora
Persephone	Proserpine
Eris	Discordia
Poseidon	Neptune
Eros	Cupid
Rhea	Ops
Hades	Pluto
Zeus	Jupiter
Hephaestus	Vulcan

AENEAS: THE TROJAN HERO

Aeneas's Journey to Italy

Ⓡ

The Romans didn't borrow everything from the Greeks, of course. They had their own stories about the beginnings of their culture and the founding of their city. The Romans believed that their ancestor was the Trojan hero Aeneas.

Aeneas was one of the few who survived the Trojan War. He was the leader of those Trojans who managed to escape the war with their lives. With their city destroyed, the Trojans needed a new home. They wandered, unable to find a suitable place, until they received a prophecy that they should make their home in the place of their "ancient mother." At first, the prophecy was interpreted as referring to Crete, but when the displaced Trojans went there, they suffered a famine. They had to reconsider the prophecy.

The prophecy referred to Italy, the homeland of Dardanus, an ancestor of the Trojans. So the Trojans set out for Italy, but their journey was not an easy one. They suffered terrible sea storms and an encounter with Harpies—and they had Juno to deal with.

JUNO'S ANGER

Juno (you've known her throughout this book as Hera) could be ruthless, especially when she took things personally. Juno had favored the Greeks during the Trojan War and saw no reason to change her mind about the Trojans after the war had ended. One of the reasons she hated the Trojans was that Dardanus, their ancestor, was the illegitimate son of Jupiter (the Greek Zeus) and Electra—and Juno's anger at her husband's extramarital affairs could last for generations.

Juno wanted the Trojans to fail and tried to prevent them from finding a new home. First, she tried to make the winds destroy the Trojans' ships. But without the cooperation of Neptune (Poseidon), little damage was done. In fact, angry that Juno had invaded his domain, Neptune stopped the storm, but the winds had already blown the Trojan fleet far off course.

Trying to get back on course, the fleet made numerous stops. During a stop in Carthage, the queen, Dido, fell in love with Aeneas and committed suicide when he left her.

Many of the Trojans, who had been wandering for years, grew tired of traveling and wanted to settle down. Juno incited some of the women to mutiny. When the fleet stopped in Sicily, Juno convinced the women to set fire to the ships. Some ships were destroyed, but Jupiter intervened to save the rest. Even with a reduced fleet, Aeneas refused to give up his quest for a new homeland. The remaining ships couldn't carry everyone, so he allowed some of the refugees to stay in Sicily, but the others continued with him on the journey.

REACHING ITALY

Finally, more than seven years after the fall of Troy, Aeneas and his companions landed in Italy. Now that they'd reached their destination, however, they weren't sure what to do next. Until this point, Aeneas had relied on visions and prophecies, but now he needed further guidance.

Aeneas decided to travel to the Underworld and seek advice from his father's shade. In the Elysian Fields he met his father, who told him that he would found the Roman race and his descendants would found the city of Rome.

Aeneas returned to the world of the living and set out again. This time, he and his followers landed in Latium, a region on the Tiber River. Latium was ruled by King Latinus, a son of Faunus (Pan). He had received an oracle saying that his daughter, Lavinia, would marry a man from abroad. Latinus recognized Aeneas as the man whose arrival the oracle had foretold, so the Trojans received a warm welcome.

JUNO INTERVENES AGAIN

Of course, Juno couldn't leave it alone. She decided to stir up trouble between the Trojans and the Latins by taking advantage of a prearranged marriage between Lavinia and Turnus, king of the Rutulians. King Latinus and his wife, Amata, had already promised their daughter in marriage to Turnus, who also happened to be Amata's nephew. Oracle or no, he wasn't willing to be pushed aside for some stranger.

Juno sent a Fury to turn Amata against a marriage between Aeneas and Lavinia. Next, the Fury incited Turnus to declare war.

The Death of Turnus

Aeneas did not kill Turnus right away. When it became evident that Aeneas had won the fight, Turnus begged for mercy. Aeneas almost conceded, but then he saw that Turnus wore the sword belt of a friend of his who'd been killed. Aeneas killed Turnus on the spot.

The Trojans fought valiantly against the Rutulians. Many casualties occurred on both sides. Because each commander was losing so many men, the two leaders agreed to solve the dispute through one-on-one combat. Aeneas was a better fighter than Turnus, and Juno knew this. She persuaded Turnus to back out of the agreement at the last minute.

Furious, Aeneas launched a vicious attack on the Rutulians. So many men were killed that Turnus was rumored to be among the slain. Distraught over her nephew's death, Amata killed herself.

Turnus, however, had not died. Once again, the two leaders agreed to meet in single combat. This time, Juno was nowhere to be seen. Aeneas easily defeated Turnus and ended the war.

ROMULUS, REMUS, AND THE CREATION OF ROME

Exploring the Origins of the Romans

Ⓡ

Following the war with the Rutulians, Aeneas negotiated terms with the Latins, who agreed to follow the Trojans' rule and worship their gods. In return, the Trojans agreed to call themselves Latins and learn the Latin language.

Aeneas fulfilled the oracle's prophecy and married Lavinia. They had a son named Silvius, the first child born of the Roman race. However, Silvius did not succeed his father as ruler of Latium. Aeneas had a son from his first marriage named Ascanius, whose name later changed to Iulus.

Iulus wandered inland and founded a city called Alba Longa, which would become the capital of the Latins and remain so for many years. Each new ruler of Latium took his place on the throne in Alba Longa. Throughout the first twelve generations of rulers (all descendants of Aeneas), the Latins enjoyed peace and prosperity.

It was this combination of Trojans and Latins that would begin the new Roman race. However, they weren't called Romans yet—because there wasn't yet a city named Rome.

PEACE DISTURBED

Although the Latins enjoyed a peaceful succession of rulers for several generations, that contentment ended when Numitor ascended the throne. Numitor's rule was usurped by his brother, Amulius, who took steps to ensure no one would challenge him. Amulius killed Numitor's two sons and forced his only daughter, Rhea Silvia, to become a Vestal Virgin.

Rhea Silvia became pregnant and gave birth to twin boys—though a Vestal Virgin, she was unable to protect herself from the amorous advances of Mars (Ares). Furious at this threat to his power, Amulius had Rhea Silvia imprisoned and ordered his servants to drown the two boys in a nearby river. The servants couldn't bring themselves to kill the two helpless infants, however, and set them adrift instead.

Even though the servants didn't drown the boys, the children surely would have died if Mars hadn't come to their rescue. Mars sent a wolf to suckle the infants, and after they were weaned, he sent a woodpecker to bring them food. Eventually, a shepherd named Faustulus found them, took them home, and raised them in secret.

Who was Faustulus?

Faustulus was King Amulius's chief shepherd. Even though Faustulus served the king and suspected that these were the children Amulius had ordered killed, he braved the penalty for treason and raised the two boys as his own.

The boys, named Romulus and Remus, grew up well educated, strong, and brave. They were friends with the local shepherds, who looked to the two young men as their leaders. Their foster father eventually revealed the details of their infancy, and told them of his suspicions that they were Rhea Silvia's lost twins and therefore heirs to the throne.

After Romulus and Remus had discovered their true identity, they visited Numitor and formed a plan to remove Amulius from the throne. The brothers organized a rebellion with the support of their shepherd friends and those who remained faithful to Numitor. They killed Amulius and returned Numitor to his throne.

FOUNDING THE CITY OF ROME

Romulus and Remus were too adventurous to sit back and wait for their inheritance, so they ventured out to found their own city. They agreed on a location (on the Tiber River near the site of their rescue by the wolf), but that's where their agreements ended. They argued over every other detail: Who would oversee the design of the city? Who would name it? And most important, who would rule?

Since they couldn't agree about any of these matters, the brothers turned to the gods, asking for an omen to settle their dispute. Each man positioned himself on a hill overlooking the location they'd chosen. Remus saw the six vultures, and then Romulus saw twelve vultures. Each proclaimed himself the winner: Remus saw the birds first, but Romulus saw more birds. The argument became heated and a fight broke out. Remus was killed, and Romulus became the ruler of the new city and named it Rome after himself.

BRINGING WOMEN TO ROME

Romulus needed to populate his city, so he encouraged fugitives and runaways to take refuge in Rome. The city's population grew quickly, but there was a problem—virtually no women lived there, because no man from the surrounding area would allow his daughter to marry the rogues who inhabited Rome. Romulus decided he would have to take women by force.

He planned a great festival, complete with games and theatrical performances, and invited everyone to attend. Once the guests were inside the city, the Romans barred its gates. They attacked their guests, seizing the women and girls, and wounding or killing the men and boys. Once they had a good supply of women, they drove the remaining men out of the city.

The kidnapped women were terrified, but Romulus made a great speech to soothe and reassure them. He won over the women, who became content to stay in Rome.

Of course, the men weren't willing to give up their wives and daughters so easily, and several attacks were made on Rome. Most of the attacks were disorganized and mounted by small bands of men, and the Romans had little difficulty in repelling them. But the Sabine tribe was a different story.

The Sabine men banded together and organized themselves with a strategic plan of attack. Under their king, Titus Tatius, the Sabine men blockaded the city and bribed the daughter of a Roman commander to open the gates to the citadel. When the Sabine men seemed to be winning, the abducted women put themselves and their children between the two armies. The fighting stopped—no one on either side wanted to harm the women, and of course, the women did not want to see their Sabine fathers or their new Roman husbands harmed.

Unable to continue fighting without killing the very thing they were fighting for, the two armies had no choice but to call a truce. The two sides agreed to merge their populations to create a single federation. Romulus and Titus Tatius would rule jointly.

THE DEATH OF ROMULUS

Romulus and Titus Tatius expanded the Roman kingdom and built a powerful army. The city was growing and flourishing in peace. Then, after nearly forty years as a successful ruler, Romulus suddenly disappeared.

During one of Romulus's routine inspections of his army on the Campus Martius, a violent thunderstorm occurred. Romulus was surrounded by a cloud and vanished from sight.

An Ancient Conspiracy Theory

Not everyone believed this account of Romulus's disappearance. Some thought a group of conspirators had murdered the king: As a storm cloud moved in and hid them from view, some senators murdered the king and tore his body to pieces. When the storm broke, the men threw the king's remains into the strong winds, which scattered the pieces.

Those who witnessed his disappearing act claimed that the gods had reached down and lifted Romulus into the heavens. Most of Rome accepted this as truth and honored Romulus's divinity. He was thereafter worshiped as Quirinus, a god of war.

THE ROMAN KINGS

The Age of Kings

ℝ

After Romulus disappeared, six other kings rose to power in Rome. Each played a role in expanding the city and making the city's influence known throughout the world.

NUMA POMPILIUS

Numa was the son-in-law of Titus Tatius. A peaceful man, Numa was known as "the Lawgiver." He instituted new laws and kept the peace with neighboring cities and tribes. Celebrated for his wisdom and piety, Numa credited his mistress, the nymph Egeria, with giving him counsel. Although Numa would propose new laws, it was said he would not introduce them until Egeria had given them her approval.

TULLUS HOSTILIUS

After Numa came Tullus Hostilius. Whereas Numa had championed peace, Tullus was more interested in expansion. He worked hard to train and exercise Rome's army—and his hard work paid off. Under Tullus's rule, Rome conquered several cities and gained a reputation as a formidable power. Tullus also conquered Alba Longa and forced its people to live in Rome, which doubled Rome's population.

A Severe Punishment for Disrespect

It was bad enough to neglect the gods in the first place. But it was worse to follow up that neglect with an insincere attempt to win the gods' favor. From the gods' point of view, death was the only punishment for such a show of disrespect.

For thirty-two years, Rome's expansion was his main concern. Unfortunately, Tullus neglected to pay proper tribute to the gods, so they sent a plague to Rome. Ill and near death, Tullus tried to appease the gods, but it was too late: A lightning strike finished him off.

ANCUS MARCIUS

Ancus Marcius, Numa's grandson, inherited his grandfather's preference for peace. This king was best known for building the first wooden bridge over the Tiber River. He also established Ostia as a port at the Tiber's mouth.

Although known as a peaceful ruler, Ancus, like his predecessors, did expand the kingdom of Rome. He pushed the city boundaries farther south and west, gaining the land of Latium.

LUCIUS TARQUINIUS PRISCUS

Lucius Tarquinius Priscus was an Etruscan who had no blood right to the throne. But he changed his name to Lucius Tarquinius Priscus (from the Etruscan name Lucumo) and made himself indispensable to King Ancus. When the king died, Tarquinius was elected king despite the fact Ancus had left behind two sons.

Tarquinius ruled for thirty-eight years and was credited with several improvements to Rome. He expanded the kingdom even more, conquering several Latin towns. He began the construction of a temple to Jupiter and a great stone wall to surround the city. He is also believed to have drained the marshy land that would later become the Roman Forum.

The sons of Ancus never forgave Tarquinius for taking the throne. They felt they were the rightful rulers of Rome and hired two shepherds to murder him.

SERVIUS TULLIUS

Servius Tullius was the child of one of the queen's slaves. The queen recognized the child's greatness, however, and worked with Tarquinius to ensure that the child would succeed to the throne. When Servius was of age, he married Tarquinius's daughter, becoming next in line to rule.

A Conniving Daughter

Some myths say that Servius's daughter was the mastermind behind the plot to overthrow her father. When Servius was killed, Superbus would not allow a burial, and Servius's daughter drove her carriage over her father's corpse.

Servius was a successful ruler, admired and respected by the people of Rome. Like his predecessors, he expanded the kingdom; he also built a wall, called the Servian Wall, around the perimeter of the city. He was said to have divided the citizens into classes based on ownership of property and introduced the worship of Diana (Artemis).

Servius was murdered by his son-in-law, Lucius Tarquinius Superbus, who wanted the throne. Legend has it that Superbus forced Servius from his throne and threw him out of the Senate House. He then sent assassins to stab Servius to death.

LUCIUS TARQUINIUS SUPERBUS

Compared to his predecessors, Lucius Tarquinius Superbus was a poor ruler. He had no interest in winning the people's respect; he merely wanted power. For twenty-five years, he hung on to his throne through a reign of terror. He expanded Rome's kingdom by conquering several Latin states and Rutulian towns. His son Sextus, who would have been the next king, caused an uproar that led to the end of the monarchy.

Sextus was every bit as ruthless as his father, taking whatever he wanted with little regard for anyone else. One night he decided he wanted his friend's wife, Lucretia. While her husband was away, Sextus visited Lucretia's home and made advances to her. Lucretia rejected him, but Sextus threatened to dishonor her family by claiming he found Lucretia and her servant in bed together. Fearing for her family's honor, Lucretia gave in.

When her husband returned, Lucretia told him the whole story. Lucretia made her husband, her father, and a friend, Lucius Junius Brutus, swear that they would avenge her death, and then she killed herself. The men gathered a small army of rebels and killed Sextus. They drove Superbus from Rome and abolished the monarchy. This was the beginning of the Roman Republic.

MODERN-DAY MYTHOLOGY

Encountering Myths in Everyday Life

G R

One way that the ancient myths of Greece and Rome live on is in the English language. Many words and phrases have their origins in classical mythology. Earlier sections have mentioned some of these terms; this section describes others you might recognize.

COMMON WORDS AND PHRASES

Here are a few words and phrases that originated in classical mythology:

- An *odyssey* is a long, often difficult journey filled with adventures—just like Odysseus's trip home from Troy.
- The word *panic*, which means a sudden, overwhelming fear, traces its origins back to the god Pan. During battle, Pan would let out a terrifying shriek that made the enemy frantic with fear.
- An *arachnid* is a spider. This word comes from Arachne, the mortal woman who foolishly challenged Athena to a weaving contest and was transformed into a spider.
- A *phobia* is a fear, often an irrational one. The word comes from Phobos, a son of Ares who caused terror on the battlefield.
- The word *aphrodisiac* refers to a food or potion that causes sexual desire. The section "Aphrodite" describes how Aphrodite liked to stir up sexual desire among both mortals and immortals.

- An *Adonis* is a handsome young man—just like the Adonis who was loved by Aphrodite.
- When someone is consistently lucky, that person is said to have *the Midas touch*. As in the myth of King Midas, everything the person touches turns to gold.
- Hermaphroditus, a son of Hermes and Aphrodite, merged physically with a nymph, becoming both male and female. Today, the word *hermaphrodite* refers to an animal or person born with both male and female sex organs.
- The element *titanium*, which takes its name from the Titans, is known for its strength. *Titanic* means gigantic and powerful, just like the ancient Titans.
- Another element with a mythological name is *mercury* (the Roman name for Hermes). A person with a *mercurial* nature is quick-witted, lively, and volatile.
- The names of several months come from Roman mythology: *January* is named for Janus, a double-faced god of doorways and beginnings; *March* is named for Mars, the god of war; *April* may come from a variant of Aphrodite; *May*'s name comes from Maia, an earth goddess; and *June* is named in honor of Juno. Although many of the days of the week take their names from Norse mythology, *Saturday* is named in honor of the Roman god Saturn.

Psychology draws some of its terms from classical mythology. For example, *narcissism*, a personality disorder characterized by excessive self-love, draws its name from the story of Narcissus, found in "Achilles, Agamemnon, and Other Important Heroes." Psychoanalysis teaches that people have two drives, one toward life and one toward death; these drives are sometimes referred to as the *Eros instinct* (life) and the *Thanatos instinct* (death).

Psychology's Ancient Connection

The word *psychology* has its roots in Greek myth. *Psyche* means mind, soul, or spirit, but Psyche was also a mythological character who had a love affair with Eros, the god of love.

Probably the most famous psychological term derived from classical mythology came from Sigmund Freud, the Austrian neurologist who founded psychoanalysis. Freud coined the phrase *Oedipal complex* based on the myth of Oedipus, which you also read about in "Achilles, Agamemnon, and Other Important Heroes." An oracle proclaimed that Oedipus would kill his father and marry his mother, and Freud believed that these feelings of jealousy toward the same-sex parent and love for the opposite-sex parent were a phase that all children go through.

The world of sports also has references to classical mythology. The *Olympic Games*, which began in ancient Greece, are the most obvious example. *Nike*, a popular brand of athletic shoes, is the name of the Greek goddess of victory. And the word *marathon* comes from the myth of Pheidippides, an Athenian messenger. During the Battle of Marathon, Pheidippides ran from Athens to Sparta to ask the Spartans to join the Athenians in repelling an invasion. To get from Athens to Sparta, Pheidippides ran about 140 miles in under two days—then had to run the 140 miles back to Athens with the Spartans' reply.

Olympic Honor

Today's Olympic Games are a variation on the festivals held in ancient Greece to honor the gods. During these festivals, sports and artistic contests were held. Even then, winning an event in the Olympic Games was an admirable and respected feat.

References to myths can appear where you least expect them, such as in the world of computer science. In general usage, a *Trojan horse*—just like the one that led to the defeat of Troy—is something that appears desirable but in fact presents a threat. In computer science, a Trojan horse (often called a Trojan for short) is a computer program that looks useful and innocent, such as a free computer game, but allows unauthorized access to your computer.

Written in the Stars

Throughout this book are stories of heroes and other mortals who were honored by the gods after death by being turned into constellations. Other constellations include Ursa Major and Ursa Minor (Callisto and her son Arcas, whose stories appear in "Artemis"; more on Callisto can also be found in "Zeus's Many Affairs"); Andromeda, Perseus, and Cetus (see "Perseus"); and Hercules (see "The Twelve Labors of Heracles"—the Greek Heracles became the Roman Hercules).

The zodiac signs also come from classical mythology:

- *Aries* is the golden-fleeced ram.
- *Taurus* is the white bull that carried Europa to Crete.

- *Gemini* is Castor and Pollux, twin sons of Zeus and Leda.
- *Cancer* is the crab that Heracles faced.
- *Leo* is another enemy of Heracles, the Nemean Lion.
- *Virgo* is Astraea, the Roman goddess of justice.
- *Libra* represents Astraea's scales.
- *Scorpio* is the scorpion that killed Orion.
- *Sagittarius* is the Centaur Chiron, a great archer.
- *Capricorn* is the goat Amalthea, who nursed Zeus.
- *Aquarius* is Ganymede, the gods' cupbearer.
- *Pisces* is the fish that served as a disguise for both Aphrodite and Eros.

"Comparing Greek and Roman Mythologies" gives the Roman equivalents for the names of Greek gods and goddesses. Most of the planets in the solar system are named after these Roman deities. Other celestial bodies, such as some asteroids and several of Jupiter's moons, are also named for mythological figures.

APPENDIX A

Family Tree of the Greek Gods

APPENDIX B

Family Tree of the Roman Gods

INDEX